ROYAL MAIL
LINERS 1925-71
William H. Miller

AMBERLEY

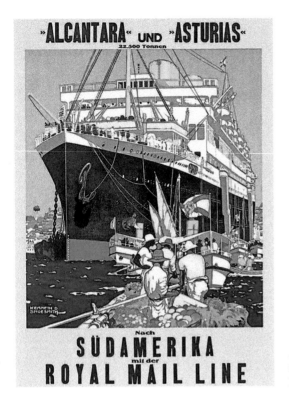

A fine Kenneth Shoesmith rendition: an inbound Royal Mail liner. (Norman Knebel Collection)

To Desmond Kirkpatrick; seaman from a bygone age,
avid traveler, staff member at Royal Mail Lines

Front Cover: The *Andes* at Southampton.
Rear Cover: The *Alcantara* at sea. (Both paintings by Stephen Card)

First published 2017

Amberley Publishing
The Hill, Stroud
Gloucestershire, GL5 4EP

www.amberley-books.com

Copyright © William H. Miller, 2017

The right of William H. Miller to be identified as the Author of this work has been asserted in accordance with the Copyrights, Designs and Patents Act 1988.

ISBN 978 1 4456 6127 8 (print)
ISBN 978 1 4456 6128 5 (ebook)

British Library Cataloguing in Publication Data.
A catalogue record for this book is available from the British Library.

Typeset in 10pt on 13pt Celeste.
Typesetting by Amberley Publishing.
Printed in the UK.

Contents

Acknowledgments   4

Foreword   5

Introduction   6

1. South American Sensations: *Alcantara* and *Asturias*   8

2. Earlier Liners: *Araguaya, Avon, Asturias* (1907)/*Arcadian, Arlanza* (1912)*, Almanzora*   24

3. D Class: *Deseado, Demerara, Desna, Durro*   28

4. The 'O Ships': *Orduna, Orbita, Oropesa, Orca* and *Ohio*   29

5. 'The Highland Boats' – *Highland Monarch, Highland Chieftain, Highland Brigade,
    Highland Hope, Highland Princess* and *Highland Patriot*   32

6. Cruising on the *Atlantis* (ex-*Andes*)   42

7. The Luxurious *Andes*   52

8. Royal Mail Liners Go to War   72

9. Ship of Misfortune: *Magdalena*   79

10. 'The Three Graces' – *Amazon, Aragon* and *Arlanza* (1960)   84

11. Post Script: Long After Royal Mail   95

    Bibliography   96

Acknowledgments

Like the crew of a liner, say the *Andes*, it took many hands – crew members – to assemble and construct this book. As author, I am more like the chief purser.

First my thanks to Amberley Publishing Company and especially Connor Stait to taking on this title and seeing it through. Special thanks to Bermuda-based maritime artist Stephen Card, for his splendid covers, and to Des Kirkpatrick, who served with Royal Mail Lines and shared his recollections and insights. Then great appreciation to Norman Knebel, who shared his vast archive of ship memorabilia, especially in his vast steamship poster archive and collection of period brochures. Special thanks also to fellow author David Hutchings for his evocative foreword.

And then a team of first-class crew – a salute of gratitude to Ernest Arroyo, Michael Cassar, the late Bob Cummins, the late Frank Cronican, Gordon Dalzell, Richard de Kerbrech, John Draffin, the late Alex Duncan, Richard Faber, the late John Gillespie, Bill Harkness, Tony La Forgia, Michael D. J. Lennon, Anton Logvinenko, Hisashi Noma, the late Ron Peach, Charlie Warmington and Al Wilhelmi. Companies and organizations that have assisted include Hoegh-Ugland Car Carriers, Royal Mail Lines, Southern Newspapers Ltd, Steamship Historical Society of America, World Ocean & Cruise Liner Society and World Ship Society – especially the Port of New York Branch. Any omissions are sincerely regretted.

Foreword

As a schoolboy on the Isle of Wight in the 1950s, I had my favourite, special shipping companies whose ships that I made a point of watching as they passed through the waters of the Solent that lay between the Isle of Wight – where I then lived – and the mainland.

Ships of the Cunard, Union-Castle Line, Orient and P&O lines were all favourites with their magical names that, on all the colourful brochures that I collected, began with those enigmatic letters 'RMS' – Royal Mail Steamer; an appellation that seemed to give these ships an extra special aura.

And then there was the line that had these words in its company name – the Royal Mail Line. On my eagerly anticipated trips to Southampton with a long-standing friend, we would walk along Canute Road and visit the shipping offices there to pick up wonderfully smelling brochures. The Royal Mail Line's offices on nearby Queen's Terrace were a special place, with large gold letters around its perimeter gorgeously proclaiming to whom those offices belonged.

One of my most favourite ships was Royal Mail's *Andes*, with her beautifully proportioned black hull, gleaming white superstructure and largish buff funnel.

Then, one bright, hot, sunny day when I was walking into Cowes along the Prince's Esplanade – the tide high and the calcite-coloured sea very calm – an elderly, smokey cargo vessel was heading westwards and, as I looked over my shoulder to follow it down the western Solent, there, coming in from the west, was the beautiful *Andes*; this time painted in cruising white that gleamed in the sparkling sunshine.

Now my old friend Bill Miller's wonderful book enables me to look over my shoulder once again and relive those sunny days of Royal Mail.

David F. Hutchings
Lee-on-The Solent, October 201
Author: *RMS Caronia – Legacy of a Pretty Sister*

Introduction

Royal Mail Lines was one of the greatest names in British shipping. Although now long gone, the company deserves further attention: a nostalgic review, especially for its long line of passenger ships. They owned some very important and very interesting ships: the sisters *Alcantara* and *Asturias*; the legendary cruise ship *Atlantis*; the Highland class of six sister ships; the beautiful *Andes*, which later became one of the world's finest cruise ships; the tragedy of the *Magdalena*; and finally the *Amazon* and her two sisters – the very last three-class passenger ships in the British fleet. We begin our passenger fleet review in the mid-1920s and continue until the final cruise of the *Andes* in the spring of 1971.

But Royal Mail itself might not have existed past the early 1930s – the age of international Depression. Formed in 1839 with assistance from the British Government and a royal charter from the young Queen Victoria in the form of a subsidy to carry mail to ports around the world, it all began with no less than fourteen steamers. The primary service was twice-monthly sailings from Southampton or Falmouth to Barbados. Maritime historian and author Richard de Kerbrech noted, 'Royal Mail Lines was rather unique. They were one of only four British shipping companies to include the Crown in their house flags. The others were Pacific Steam Navigation Co., Orient Steam Navigation Co. and Elder Dempster Lines. When the monarch was a queen, like Victoria and Elizabeth II, the house flags sported the Queen's crown. With monarchs such as Edward VII, George V and George VI (and probably Edward VIII), the flag crown was changed to the King's Crown.'

By 1900, Royal Mail was a flourishing passenger ship firm, but facing increasing competition from American, as well as German, shipping lines. Consequently, there was a growing trend toward amalgamation, begun by America's J. Pierpont Morgan, who had joined railways but now looked to do the same with Atlantic shipping lines. By 1912, Morgan's IMM – the International Mercantile Marine Company – included no less than six companies: the White Star Line, American Line, Red Star Line, Atlantic Transport Line, Leyland Line and Dominion Line. Combined, there were 126 ships totalling more than 1,000,000 gross tons. But all what was not what it seemed. While 1912 was a boom year, and when 122 different British shipping firms paid dividends (averaging 7 per cent), the IMM paid no dividends at all.

Owen Philips (1863–1937), later ennobled as Lord Kylsant, controlled the Royal Mail Steam Packet Company, as it was officially called. He had joined the Line as a board member in 1903, quickly impressed everyone and, quite remarkably, was made chairman within three months. Like IMM, Royal Mail was at the head of a 'shipping empire' – one which controlled no less than twelve other lines: Pacific Steam Navigation Company, Lamport & Holt, Forwood Line, Glen Line, Shire Line, Elder Dempster, Nelson Line, Union-Castle, the British & African Steam Navigation Co., the Elder Line and the Imperial Direct West India Mail service. Altogether, the combined fleets amounted to 1,400,000 gross tons and, in fact, more than the IMM. But Lord Kylsant was wildly ambitious – as well as complex, secretive and often deceptive. The exact ownership of ships, even the largest ones, was often complex and sometimes unclear. During the First World War (1914–18), he added Moss Steamship Co. and MacAndrew's and launched Coast Lines. Then, soon after the

Armistice, in 1919, when ship prices reached an all-time high, he bought Bullard King, David MacIver Sons & Co. and J. & P. Hutchinson. During the war, the group accumulated profits of £20,000,000. In 1919, Kylsant bought seventy-seven of the British Government's surplus standardised freighters and dispersed these among his various fleets. At the same time, Harland & Wolff – the noted shipbuilder in Northern Ireland – joined the group and soon Kylsant enlarged that company's shipbuilding capacity. On the stock market, he raised a further £11,500,000 (or £350,000,000 in 2016 prices).

Although there was a shipping slump in 1920, this failed to stop Kylsant. A year later, he applied for a Government loan and continued to raise money through the new issue market. By late 1922, the Group had raised the equivalent of £1 billion, on which Kylsant was committed to paying a fixed 6 per cent. But saddled with huge interest payments and so increasingly relying on borrowed monies, the forecasts were no longer quite as bright.

Kylsant seemed undaunted, however. Next, he proceeded to buy the White Star Line (in 1927) and increase his shares in Shaw, Savill & Albion. Further shares had to be issued, another Government loan engineered and still more ships were acquired. By 1925, the Group – by then controlled by Elder Dempster Lines – consisted of 140 companies with a combined fleet of over 2,600,000 gross tons. Nearly 60,000 people were employed, both afloat and ashore. After acquiring White Star, Royal Mail was part of the biggest shipping group in the world. The biggest liners yet for Royal Mail and the Group, the *Alcantara* and *Asturias*, were ordered, but soon the balloon would burst and the Kylsant shipping empire would come dramatically crumbling down.

When the 10,500-grt Lamport & Holt liner *Vestris* foundered in November 1928, the perennial chickens came home to roost. Loans were due and repayment could not be made. The projected boom in shipping for the early 1930s that Kylsant banked on would never come. Wall Street crashed in October 1929 and the effects spread quickly, and soon throughout the world. Shipping plunged. By 1930, Kylsant's empire was like a house of cards, but a collapsing house. It all came crashing down.

The Government immediately launched an investigation, fearful of major maritime financial disaster. It was called the 'Royal Mail Case'. The Government had to guarantee help; assurance that such a mighty fleet would survive. Later found guilty of issuing a false prospectus, Kylsant himself was unseated and was sent to prison for twelve months. Quickly, corporate and financial salvage became the order of the day. The Royal Mail Steam Packet Company was soon sensibly liquidated and its assets transferred. By 1932, Royal Mail Lines Ltd – headed by Lord Essendon – was spun off as a separate company following the final dismantling of the Kylsant shipping empire. The new Royal Mail operations concentrated in South America, to the West Indies, to the Pacific coast of North America and in cruising.

Herein, we begin our passenger ship fleet review just before, in the mid-1920s. And a grand and interesting fleet it was. In these pages, the Royal Mail liners will hopefully sail again.

Bill Miller
Secaucus, New Jersey, USA
Spring 2017

1. South American Sensations: *Alcantara* and *Asturias*

Above: The romance of a great ocean liner: one of Kenneth Shoesmith's superb depictions – early evening in the tropics for the *Alcantara*. (Author's Collection)

Left: Improved appearance: the *Alcantara* at Southampton with her heightened funnels. (Author's Collection)

Above: A superb colour view of the *Alcantara* at Southampton. (Anton Logvinenko)

Right: A mighty ship: second class to South America. (Author's Collection)

Above: Cap badge from Royal Mail Lines. (Des Kirkpatrick Collection)

Left: Sailing to the sun: winter voyages to South America. (Norman Knebel Collection)

Aerial view at Southampton in 1937: the *Asturias* is in the foreground; the *Almanzora* to the left; the troopship *Dilwara* to the right. In the background (from left to right): *Britannic, Orcades, Andania* and *Berengaria*. (Royal Mail Lines)

Photograph by " The Times.

The royal yacht *Victoria & Albert* passing the *Alcantara* during the Royal Naval Review for King George V on 16 July 1935. (Royal Mail Lines)

Exotic decor: the Moorish Lounge aboard the *Asturias*. (Norman Knebel Collection)

A good book: the Reading & Writing Room on the *Alcantara*. (Norman Knebel Collection)

Another view of the
splendid Library on
the *Alcantara*. (Norman
Knebel Collection)

Refuge: the enchanting
Winter Garden aboard
the *Alcantara*. (Norman
Knebel Collection)

Left: Travel on the *Asturias*: the Second Class Salon. (Norman Knebel Collection)

Below: An artist's rendering of a very broad enclosed Promenade Deck. (Norman Knebel Collection)

ROYAL MAIL LINES, LIMITED

NAME

PASSENGERS' BAGGAGE per " "

EMBARKED   DESTINATION

STATE ROOM

Berth No. IT IS NECESSARY TO INSERT HERE THE NUMBER

Bound for South America: a baggage tag. (Author's Collection)

ROYAL MAIL
PASSENGER SERVICES
TO AND FROM
SOUTH AMERICA
BRAZIL · URUGUAY · ARGENTINA
FROM SOUTHAMPTON, LONDON AND LIVERPOOL
VIA SPAIN, PORTUGAL, MADEIRA AND LAS PALMAS

NORTH PACIFIC COAST PORTS
VIA BERMUDA, JAMAICA AND PANAMA CANAL

PLEASURE CRUISES
BY "ATLANTIS"
TO NORWAY, NORTHERN CAPITALS,
MEDITERRANEAN, ATLANTIC ISLES, ETC.

TOURS
TO BRAZIL AND ARGENTINA AND
ENCIRCLING SOUTH AMERICA
ALSO SPAIN, PORTUGAL, MADEIRA AND LAS PALMAS

ROYAL MAIL LINES, LTD.
LONDON   America House, Cockspur Street, S.W.1.   Phone : Whitehall 9646 (3 lines)
Royal Mail House, Leadenhall Street, E.C.3.   Phone : Royal 9120 (Private Bch. Exchange)
LIVERPOOL.   The Pacific Steam Navigation Company, Goree, Water Street (3).
Also at MANCHESTER, BIRMINGHAM, CARDIFF, GLASGOW AND SOUTHAMPTON
Offices and Agencies throughout the World

Printed in England   The Baynard Press.

Diversity: the many passenger
services of Royal Mail Lines in
1935. (Author's Collection)

One of the best known liner routes to South America was aboard Britain's Royal Mail Lines. 'At Royal Mail, you were trained as a steward as if in a Russian ballet school,' recalled the late Ron Peach, who served aboard no less than five Royal Mail passenger ships – the *Alcantara, Andes, Highland Monarch, Amazon* and *Aragon*. Their trade, back in the 1950s and '60s, was the UK–east coast of South America run, from either Southampton or London via Vigo (in Spain), Lisbon and Las Palmas (in the Canary Islands), across the mid-Atlantic to Rio de Janeiro, Santos, Montevideo and Buenos Aires. London to Buenos Aires took nearly three weeks on what was probably the finest ocean liner service to Latin America in its day.

Ron Peach served in first class aboard Royal Mail's otherwise three-class ships – with first, cabin and tourist class accommodations. 'You served full afternoon tea in the staterooms and suites, for example, and then returned to lay out the evening clothes, which included putting the studs in a gentlemen's dress shirts,' he recalled. 'Years later, in the early 1970s, when I joined the Cunard Line and the *Queen Elizabeth 2*, it seemed much more informal by comparison to first class on Royal Mail Lines.'

The *Asturias* and *Alcantara* were the Royal Mail as well as British 'sensations' of the 1920s. Constructed by affiliate Harland & Wolff in 1926 and 1927 respectively, they weighed in at 22,000 gross tons and measured 656 feet in length. Fitted with Danish-built Burmeister & Wain diesels, they were twin-screw ships capable of up to 17 knots. Onboard the *Asturias*, there was berthing for up to 1,410 passengers – 410 in first class, 232 in second class and 768 in third class.

By the mid-1920s, Lord Kylsant realized that competition on the South American run was increasing. The *Asturias* and *Alcantara* were Royal Mail's reaction. Kylsant was greatly strengthening its liner position. Another British firm – Blue Star Line, headed by Lord Vestey – was adding no less than five quite luxurious combination passenger-cargo ships – the *Almeda, Andalucia, Arandora, Avelona* and *Avila* – to the UK–east coast of South American trade. Watching closely from his Royal Mail offices, Kylsant referred to these new Blue Star ships simply as 'keen competition'. But he was worried. At the same time, from across the Channel, Germany's Hamburg-South America Line would add their luxurious, 27,000 grt *Cap Arcona* along with the five sister ships of the 13,600 grt *Monte Sarmiento* class. France's Compagnie Sud Atlantique was making plans for an even larger, more luxurious liner, the magnificent, 42,500 grt *L'Atlantique*, to be commissioned in the fall of 1931. Farther south, the Italians were running their Italy–South America service with the likes of the 24,200-grt *Duilio* and *Giulio Cesare*.

Both ships were both given long and interesting lives. Harland & Wolff began to favor diesel engines for ships during the First World War and, after 1919, the company itself manufactured them. Lord Kylsant was equally convinced that diesel drive was the future for merchant shipping, for freighters but also for passenger liners. And so, as Royal Mail needed to reinforce and strengthen its position on the UK–South America run, he ordered a pair of large liners in 1924. They would be the biggest, fastest and most luxurious yet for Royal Mail. The first, the *Asturias*, was launched at Belfast on 7 July 1925 and then departed from Southampton on her maiden voyage on 26 February 1926. Her twin sister, the *Alcantara*, entered service on 4 March 1927. At the time, the pair ranked as the largest motor liners in the world. That notation soon passed to Italy's 32,600 grt *Augustus*, commissioned in October 1927. Britain's largest motor liner was later the 27,600 grt *Britannic* of White Star in 1930.

With twin squat stacks and a rather low profile, the *Asturias* and *Alcantara* seemed to project the future. They were distinctive, even eye-catching in their day – and compared well when at Southampton to, say, the likes of the classic four-funnel *Olympic* and the three-funnel *Berengaria*. The low stack, low-profile look intrigued others, such as the White Star Line, which planned three squat stacks on its new superliner, the 60,000 grt *Oceanic*; due in 1932 but in fact never built due to the onset of the Depression and White Star's own financial troubles.

The *Asturias* and *Alcantara* were also very luxurious and very comfortable. A fully furnished suite (later installed aboard the *Asturias*) was displayed at the 1924–25 British Empire Exhibition at Wembley. The two ships were called the 'floating palaces to and from South America'. The public rooms in first class were on a grand scale. The two-deck high dining room was done in French Empire and the Winter Garden based on Moorish Spain. The wood-paneled Smoking Room reflected the William & Mary period while the Writing Room was in Adam style. Even the indoor pool was grand – it had marble floors and pillars.

The two liners seemed to be an immediate success. But they did in fact have one serious blemish: they both suffered from serious vibration. After the crash of the Kylsant empire, the regrouping of Royal Mail and some serious rethinking of Royal Mail ships and their operations, it was decided to extensively refit both the *Asturias* and *Alcantara*. They were both sent back to Harland & Wolff in 1934–35 and re-engined with steam turbines. At the same time, they were also given a new look: the original squat stacks were removed and replaced by two taller funnels, which altogether gave the two liners a more powerful, even dramatically larger appearance. The forward funnels were in fact dummies, but certainly added to the handsome appearances of both ships.

By the late 1930s, Royal Mail was quite an active passenger ship company – four liners on the mainline run from Southampton to South America (*Asturias, Alcantara, Arlanza* and *Almanzora*); the five Highland ships on the same route but from London; and the splendid *Atlantis* on luxury cruises. But the onset of the Second World War, in September 1939, would change everything. Those years are covered in Chapter 8.

After the Second World War, Royal Mail restarted their South American passenger service with the 25,000-ton *Andes*, built in 1939, and the rebuilt *Alcantara*. They were the company's prime ships, based at Southampton, and for a time the 669-foot-long *Andes* ranked as both the largest and most luxurious liner on the run between Europe and South America. Royal Mail also ran a separate passenger as well as cargo service out of London, using the 'Highland boats' as they were called – the *Highland Monarch, Highland Chieftain, Highland Brigade* and *Highland Princess* – which were a series of motor ships built in 1929–30, noted for their very squat stacks and split, separate superstructures. Royal Mail actually added a new combination passenger-cargo liner, the *Magdalena*, in 1949 but she was wrecked and lost on no less than her maiden voyage.

Post-war: the *Alcantara* loading at Cherbourg, but now with one funnel. (Gillespie-Faber Collection)

Brochure cover in the 1950s for the *Alcantara*. (Des Kirkpatrick Collection)

Splendor at sea: the *Alcantara*'s First Class Main Lounge in post-war decor. (Des Kirkpatrick Collection)

Writing letters: the cosy Writing Room. (Des Kirkpatrick Collection)

A good book: the First Class Library. (Des Kirkpatrick Collection)

Filled with sea water: the First Class Indoor Pool. (Des Kirkpatrick)

Rattan refuge: the Winter Garden in first class. (Des Kirkpatrick Collection)

With touches of vivid blue, the First Class Smoking Room. (Des Kirkpatrick Collection)

Delicious dining: the First Class Dining Room with a musicians' gallery at the far end. (Des Kirkpatrick Collection)

All the comforts of home: the sitting room of a first class suite aboard the *Alcantara*. (Des Kirkpatrick Collection)

A good night's sleep: the bedroom of a first class stateroom. (Des Kirkpatrick Collection)

Comfort at sea: a twin-bedded stateroom in first class. (Des Kirkpatrick Collection)

'In the 1950s, the Argentine passengers going up to England in first class on Royal Mail were all multi-millionaires, born in Argentina but with British educations, tastes and manners,' added Ron Peach. 'Often, they owned huge, 100,000 acre estancias [ranches] in Argentina, but also maintained homes in London, as well as Paris and in the English countryside. Some of them also owned half the beef that was in the ship's refrigerated cargo holds.'

'It was completely top-drawer in those days on Royal Mail,' he added. 'You were never, ever known by your Christian name, but simply as Peach. You were much like a butler in some grand house. It was all silver service in the restaurant. In fact, you could hardly lift the silver trays because they were so heavy. The food was, of course, beyond compare. There were great platters of meat and veg. We used to ring bells as a call for dinner aboard the *Alcantara* and *Andes.*'

While the *Alcantara* sailed off to a Japanese scrapyard in the summer of 1958, the *Andes* was soon converted for full-time cruising, catering to a very select 500 passengers in all first-class configuration.

The *Asturias* as seen in the early 1950s with one funnel and no aft mast. (Cronican-Arroyo Collection)

23

After a strenuous, often difficult and uncertain war career, the *Asturias* was restored as a passenger ship, under the Ministry of Transport, but with Royal Mail Lines management. She was no longer intended for regular luxury passenger service, but as an Australian migrant ship. She sailed mostly between Southampton, Suez, Fremantle, Melbourne and Sydney. In a 1949 refit, her quarters were reorganised for 160 first class, 113 third class and 1,134 dormitory/migrant class. She remained in grey colouring, but with a Royal Mail yellow funnel. A year later, she was repainted in full Royal Mail colours. She remained on the Australian run until the summer of 1953, after which she was moved into Government trooping service, mostly to and from the South Korean war zone.

The *Asturias* had a final notation to her long, diverse career. When she sailed to Faslane in Scotland to be scrapped in September 1957, she served as a set for the film *A Night To Remember*, the story of the sinking of the *Titanic*. And so, the *Asturias* had one last assignment: she portrayed the immortal White Star liner. Maritime author David Hutchings recalled that final role for the *Asturias*. 'She was being broken-up at Ward's when Bill MacQuitty hired her for the scenes of lifeboats being lowered from the *Titanic*. Previously, he had been turned down by the Shaw Savill Line for using the *Dominion Monarch*. Shaw Savill (they had had links with White Star) told Ward's: 'Have nothing to do with MacQuitty.' Instead, his scrap of paper contract was signed by the local manager at Ward's. He could use the scrap-bound *Asturias*. Bill got pupils from the Glasgow School of Art to paint the ship black (she was white) but only the section that would be in view and to paint 'clinker planking' lines on the lifeboats. For a quick shot, these lines were effective but are quite 'wonky' on closer inspection. It had also been snowing at the time of filming so the real white snow had to be swept off the decks whilst demolition went on but on the other side of the ship. The cold conditions enabled real smoky breath to be exhaled by the actors both on deck and being lowered in the lifeboats.'

2. Earlier Liners: *Araguaya, Avon, Asturias* (1907)/*Arcadian, Arlanza* (1912), *Almanzora*

Above: Valiant ship: the *Asturias* in hospital ship colouring. (Author's Collection)

Below left: South American sailings on Royal Mail in the 1920s. (Norman Knebel Collection)

Below right: Royal Mail Lines cruising in the Twenties. (Norman Knebel Collection)

Profitable times: business was obviously booming. In the decade before the First World War, Royal Mail built eight passenger ships of the so-called A Class and then five of the D Class (listed in Chapter 3). The A Class began with the 10,037 grt *Amazon*, launched at Harland & Wolff's Belfast yard in February 1906 and then setting off on her maiden run from Southampton to Rio de Janeiro, Santos, Montevideo and Buenos Aires that June. She carried up to 300 in first class, 70 in small second class and then 500 in plain, lower-deck third class. Unfortunately, she was torpedoed and sunk off the Irish coast in March 1918.

The second ship, the *Araguaya*, followed in the autumn of 1906. She had come, however, from different shipbuilders; Workman, Clark & Co. at Belfast. The 535-foot-long, 16-knot *Avon* followed in the summer of 1907. Then it was the *Asturias* in the winter of 1908. By then, however, third class quarters had largely increased to as many as 1,200 berths.

The second group of four liners in this A Class were added after a four year gap, beginning with the *Arlanza* in September 1912. Harland & Wolff at Belfast created each of them. She and her sisters were slightly larger, at 15,000 tons, and had berthing arranged as 400 in first class, 230 second class and 760 third class. The second ship, the 589-foot-long *Andes*, was actually intended for the Pacific Steam Navigation Company, for service from Liverpool to the west coast of South America. But plans changed by her launching, in May 1908, when the ship was transferred to Royal Mail. The *Alcantara*, the third ship, arrived just weeks before the First World War dramatically erupted in the summer of 1914. The fourth, the *Almanzora*, was too late – she was completed as a Royal Navy auxiliary cruiser in the autumn of 1915.

The First World War certainly created problems – and losses. On 29 February 1916, while in the Skagerrak, the *Alcantara* – restyled as an auxiliary cruiser – intercepted the German cruiser *Greif*, which was disguised as a Norwegian vessel. As the *Alcantara* attempted to lower her boats, the *Greif* suddenly hoisted her German colours and opened fire on the unsuspecting *Alcantara*. The two ships were only 3,000 yards apart and so nearly every shot was on target. Her sister *Andes*, also an auxiliary cruiser, was nearby and came to assist. But the *Alcantara* was badly damaged and soon began to sink. Sixty-nine of her crew perished. In the end, the *Andes* sank the *Greif* (with the help of two Royal Naval vessels, the cruiser *Comus* and the destroyer *Munster*) and then rescued the survivors.

Just over a year later, on 20 March 1917, the *Asturias* was torpedoed by a German U-boat while in the English Channel. Thirty-five of her complement perished. The badly damaged ship was put under tow and ran aground off Bolt Head and abandoned. Later, the British Admiralty bought the rights to the wreck.

Previously, while being used as a hospital ship, the *Asturias* also had a special notation during the First World War. On the late afternoon of 1 February 1915, it was reported that a German submarine fired a torpedo at the ship some fifteen miles north-east of the Le Havre lightship. Fortunately, the torpedo missed its mark, but did not alter the enemy's intention, which was a flagrant violation of the Hague Convention (to which Germany subscribed) making hospital ships inviolable. Painted in all-white and with large red crosses painted along her sides and while also flying the Red Cross flag, the *Asturias* was clearly marked.

Used as an ammunition depot and all but a wreck, the *Asturias* was actually resold to Royal Mail after the war ended, in 1919, and later towed to Harland & Wolff at Belfast. Repair work was delayed, however, and the ship sat idle for three additional years. Finally, in 1922–23, she was rebuilt and restored, becoming the all-first-class cruise ship *Arcadian*. She endured for another seven years, until being laid-up at Southampton in October 1930. Three years later, she sailed off to Japan and the scrappers.

On 17 July 1920, it had been reported in the British press that after strenuous war service, the *Arlanza* was resuming normal passenger service to Brazil and the River Plate. The report was encouraging to potential passengers. She also signalled a return to luxury travel. Her first class dining saloon could seat 400 at one time. An adjoining children's dining area was separated by a movable glass screen. To ensure comfort, beds instead of bunks had been installed in many first class cabins. Added amenities include a gymnasium, children's playroom, elevator, travel office and hair-dressing salon.

The other A Class ships gave sterling service. In most cases, their fates in the end were the scrappers. The *Araguaya* was the exception. After becoming a 365-passenger cruise ship in 1926, she was sold off by Royal Mail to Dubrovnik-based Jugoslavenski Lloyd in November 1930, becoming the *Kraljica Marija* for Mediterranean and Black Sea cruising. With the onset of the Second World War, she was sold again, in 1940, to the French Government and renamed *Savoie*. Used on the South American run under the management of the Compagnie Generale Transatlantique, she was sunk on 8 November 1942 while off Casablanca during the Allied landings.

The *Avon*, briefly renamed *Avoca* during the First World War, was used mostly for cruising in the 1920s. She was scrapped by Ward's at Briton Ferry in the winter of 1930. The 1912-built *Arlanza* endured for twenty-six years until she was broken up at Blyth in 1938. The *Andes*, which became the *Atlantis* (qv) in 1930, lasted until going the breakers at Faslane in 1952. She was the longest lasting of this A Class: her career spanned thirty-nine years.

The last of these ships, the 589-foot-long *Almanzora*, completed in 1915, endured until 1948. She was broken-up at Blyth.

3. D Class: *Deseado, Demerara, Desna, Durro*

Built by Harland & Wolff at Belfast in 1911–12 – at the same time the immortal *Titanic* was being built and at the same yard – these five sister ships (the fifth, the *Drina*, was torpedoed and sunk in March 1917) were in fact quite ordinary vessels. They were, from the start, created for the migrant trade to South America and to return to Britain with Argentine beef. The 11,477 grt *Deseado* was the lead ship, being launched on 11 October 1911 and then setting off on its maiden voyage from Liverpool to ports along the east coast of South America on 5 July 1912. At 517 feet in length, she was topped by a tall, single funnel and had five cargo holds. Her passenger quarters were divided between 95 in first class, 40 in second class and, the most profitable, up to 860 in very austere third class. The migrants boarded in Portuguese and Spanish ports on the southward sailings. The *Demerara* followed two months later and then the *Desna* and the *Durro*. The *Durro* was slightly different: she had actually been built for the Imperial Direct Line; an arm of the Elder Dempster Group, but completely owned by Royal Mail. Actual Royal Mail registry did not come, quite curiously, until years later.

These ships were not requisitioned during the First World War, but instead kept on the South American run so as to deliver much needed beef to Britain. These D Ships soldiered on afterward and throughout the 1920s, but were victims of the Depression of the early 1930s. At just over twenty years of age, in 1933–34, they sailed out to Japan and the shipbreakers.

 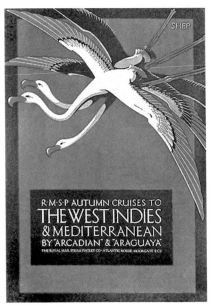

Above left: Sailing to South America on ships of the 'O Class'. (Norman Knebel Collection)

Above right: Cruising to distant lands in the 1920s. (Norman Knebel Collection)

4. The 'O Ships': *Orduna, Orbita, Oropesa, Orca* and *Ohio*

Right: Transatlantic on Royal Mail in the mid-1920s. (Norman Knebel Collection)

Below: A postcard rendition of the *Orca*. (Author's Collection)

R.M.S.P. "ORCA" (TRIPLE SCREW 16,063 TONS.)

The *Oropesa* at Santos.
(Author's Collection)

Cabin class transatlantic service in the 1920s.
(Norman Knebel Collection)

Just after the First World War, in 1920, and when more than a third of all pre-war transatlantic passenger ships had been destroyed, Royal Mail saw a gap; an opening for what might be a new, profitable passenger service. After all, almost all of the German liners (from the Hamburg America Line and North German Lloyd) were gone, if temporarily. Consequently, it was decided that Royal Mail's North Atlantic service would begin at Hamburg and then call at Southampton and Cherbourg en route to New York. From 'within the family', from Pacific Steam Navigation, Royal Mail acquired the 15,500-ton sisters *Orduna* and *Orbita*. Both were Harland & Wolff-built ships, dating from 1914–15, and very similar to Royal Mail's own A Class of liners. They each had quarters for approximately 1,120 passengers – 240 in first class, 180 in second class and, largely for westbound immigrants, 700 in third class. In 1923, for North Atlantic service, the berthing was altered to 190 first class, 221 second class and 476 third class.

Business seemed to prosper, at least in the initial years. The slightly smaller *Oropesa*, also from Pacific Steam, was added for a time, until 1923. In fact, 1922 was a particularly busy year and so Lamport & Holt's *Vestris*, *Vauban* and *Vandyck*, all normally routed to South America, were briefly chartered to make Atlantic crossings.

Success and profit and therefore encouragement continued such that, in January 1923, the 16,000 grt *Orca* was added. She was the largest ship yet on Royal Mail's New York run. Intended to be a large freighter, she was completed as a passenger ship by Harland & Wolff in 1918. Then there was the last ship on this run; the 19,000 grt *Ohio*. She was intended to be the *München* for North German Lloyd, due in 1914–15, but then was all but ignored during the First World War. Finally launched in March 1920, she was allocated to Britain under post-war reparations, was assigned to Royal Mail and renamed, but then took another three years to complete. As the *Ohio*, she was also Royal Mail's finest and fastest ship on its North Atlantic service. Altogether, she could carry 1,442 passengers – divided as 229 in first class, 523 second class and 690 third class. With a top speed of 17 knots, the *Ohio* could do Southampton to New York in eight days; the other O Ships took ten days.

All seemed to be well with this added Royal Mail arm. The service was promoted as the 'Comfort Route', offering 'high standard accommodation, food and service but all at reasonable prices'. But beginning in 1923, German shipping lines began to revive – namely the Hamburg America Line with its brand new, 20,800 grt, 1,551-passenger *Albert Ballin* and *Deutschland* in 1923–24, and the North German Lloyd with their 32,500 grt, 1,725-passenger *Columbus* in 1924. Even American ship-owners, particularly the newly established United States Lines, offered competition. By 1924–25, business for Royal Mail began to wane.

Service from Hamburg was in fact dropped in 1925. But there were experimentally extended alternative sailings from Southampton and Cherbourg – to Halifax, Quebec City and even via Bermuda. The *Orbita*, *Orca* and *Ohio* were now also spending more time in alternative service: winter, off-season cruising. In January 1927, however, when Royal Mail acquired White Star Line – which was well-established on the North Atlantic to and from New York – Royal Mail pulled out. White Star – with the likes of the big express liners *Majestic*, *Olympic* and *Homeric* – was much better known. Barely in service to South America, it was in fact the brand new *Asturias* that made the final Royal Mail Southampton–New York crossing in April 1927.

The *Ohio* and *Orca* were soon transferred to White Star, becoming the *Albertic* and *Calgaric* respectively. Both ships were victims of the Depression in the early 1930s, however. The eleven-year-old ex-*Ohio* was sold to Japanese breakers in the autumn of 1934. The thirteen-year-old former *Orca* was broken up at Rosyth in 1935. The *Orbita* and *Orduna* was returned to Pacific Steam Navigation Co. service and then resumed sailings between Liverpool, the Caribbean and ports along the west coast of South America. The *Orduna* was scrapped at Dalmuir in 1951; the *Orbita* at Newport the year before.

5. 'The Highland Boats' – *Highland Monarch, Highland Chieftain, Highland Brigade, Highland Hope, Highland Princess* and *Highland Patriot*

Bound for Brazil and Argentina: Nelson Line to South America in the early 1930s. (Author's Collection)

Above: Atlantic seawater flowing into the aft decks of the ill-fated *Highland Hope*. (Author's Collection)

Right: The Highland ships were very popular in the 1930s. (Norman Knebel Collection)

ROYAL MAIL

LONDON AND
SOUTH AMERICA
BRAZIL · URUGUAY & ARGENTINA

REGULAR FORTNIGHTLY SAILINGS
BY NEW MOTOR LINERS
"HIGHLAND BRIGADE"
"HIGHLAND CHIEFTAIN"
"HIGHLAND MONARCH"
"HIGHLAND PATRIOT"
"HIGHLAND PRINCESS"

SUNSHINE TOURS
TO SPAIN   PORTUGAL
AND CANARY ISLANDS

ROYAL MAIL LINES, LTD.
FOR FURTHER PARTICULARS APPLY WITHIN

Brochure cover for four of the Highland sisters. (Des Kirkpatrick Collection)

Post-war: the *Highland Monarch* outbound in the English Channel. (Royal Mail Lines)

The Second Class Main Lounge aboard the *Highland Monarch* in the 1950s. (Des Kirkpatrick Collection)

Tudor style: the First Class Dining Room. (Des Kirkpatrick Collection)

Inviting: the First Class Smoking Room. (Des Kirkpatrick Collection)

A first class single. (Des Kirkpatrick Collection)

A double-bedded stateroom, also in first class. (Des Kirkpatrick Collection)

The First Class Card Room. (Des Kirkpatrick Collection)

Controlled by Royal Mail from just before the First World War, in 1913, the Nelson Line also served South American east-coast ports, but from London as well as Liverpool. However, Nelson offered cheaper fares in less luxurious but comfortable quarters and so was not considered a very serious competitor but instead an alliance to Royal Mail itself. In the high pitch of the pre-Depression late 1920s, Nelson decided to jump forward with its largest passenger-cargo liners – a class of five 14,000 ton sister ships. Typically, they would come from Harland & Wolff at Belfast and, being diesel-driven, would have the low, squat stack look of the larger *Asturias* and *Alcantara*. Already they seemed like Royal Mail fleetmates, but in fact wore Nelson Line colours on their funnels. That was changed, however, in 1932, when Royal Mail and other former Kylsant companies had to be reorganised and more sensibly operated. Nelson was incorporated fully into Royal Mail in 1932, the Nelson name disappeared and these five Nelson ships were repainted with Royal Mail colours.

The 544-foot-long *Highland Monarch* was the first of the five, arriving in October 1928. She was followed in succession by the *Highland Chieftain* (in February 1929), *Highland Brigade* (in April 1929), *Highland Hope* (January 1930) and finally the *Highland Princess* (February 1930). Unfortunately, the career of the virtually brand-new *Highland Hope* was in fact very short-lived. In the early morning of 19 November 1930, during a dense fog, the South America-bound liner ran onto the rocks off the Farilhoes, near Peniche, on the coast of Portugal. The Fariloes Lighthouse was said to be not working, owing to an explosion some months before. The ship's officers and crew acted, it was later reported, with great calm and care. All of the 519 passengers as well as the 145 crew were landed in lifeboats, which were towed by Portuguese fishermen. One Spanish emigrant was injured and died later in hospital, however. Among the noted first class passengers was the Dowager Duchess of Hamilton. The British Ambassador in Lisbon later made a public statement of appreciation to all those who gave assistance to the stricken ship. Sadly, the *Highland Hope* was a complete loss and was later demolished where she laid.

A sixth ship, a replacement for the *Highland Hope*, was added in May 1932. She was completed as the *Highland Patriot*.

These Highland ships were designed to carry just over 700 passengers – 135 in first class, 66 in second class and 500 in third class. Altogether, they were unpretentious passenger ships and marketed by Royal Mail as having 'fares to suit every purse' (including austere, lower-deck third class quarters).

The extent of the company's sailings might be exemplified by this schedule from South America homeward to the UK for Dec 1931 – Jan 1932:

Demerara	Dec 1st	From Rio
Arlanza	Dec 3rd	From Santos
Highland Brigade	Dec 8th	From Santos
Asturias	Dec 17th	From Santos
Highland Hope	Dec 22nd	From Santos
Darro	Dec 29th	From Rio
Almanzora	Jan 3rd	From Santos

Highland Monarch	Jan 5th	From Santos
Deseado	Jan 12th	From Rio
Alcantara	Jan 14th	From Santos
Highland Chieftain	Jan 19th	From Santos
Desna	Jan 26th	From Rio

During the Second World War, these five Highland ships were expectedly called to duty. Unfortunately, the newest – the *Highland Patriot* – was torpedoed and sunk off Bishops Rock on 1 October 1940. Consequently, after the war, in 1948–49, Royal Mail built a replacement fifth ship; the ill-fated *Magdalena* (qv). But she was designed in a different, more contemporary style.

'They were not just the best, but very best years of my life,' remembered eighty-eight-year-old Mike Hall. 'I served in the 1950s with the Royal Mail Lines. Mostly, I was aboard the *Andes*. A beautiful ship in every way. She was the flagship of British liner service to the east coast of South America. Alternately, the *Reina Del Pacifico* looked after the west coast run. On the *Andes*, we'd sail down to Rio and Buenos Aires. A wonderful run. We'd have millionaires in first class. Some brought along their own servants, even their own cars and drivers. We also did some cruising, the occasional trip in those days. Myself, I was aboard for the six-week winter cruise from Southampton to the Caribbean in 1954. I also sailed in some of the smaller Highland ships – the *Highland Monarch* and *Highland Princess*. They used the old London Docks on their long runs down to South America. They were flat looking with two, very low rising, yellow-painted funnels. They had a break in their superstructure – with the wheelhouse, bridge & officers' quarters separated from the passenger accommodation. We referred to this as the 'chastity belt' – it was supposed to keep the officers away from the passengers other than on social occasions, of course.'

Des Kirkpatrick would subsequently join London-based Royal Mail Lines, but had an initial trip beforehand. 'In 1954, I was headed for a holiday in Spain, to Madrid,' he recalled. 'But in that age before inexpensive air flights from the UK, I boarded the *Highland Brigade* at Tilbury-London and sailed to Leixoes [Oporto] in Portugal and then took the overnight train to Madrid. Then, after a week's stay in Madrid, I took another train, the 'Lusitania Express', to Lisbon. I was scheduled to return to London and my job (at the Manchester Ship Canal) onboard the *Highland Princess*. But at Lisbon, the shipping office told me that the ship was not only a day late, but was overbooked – there were no berths. I had only £5 [$20] left in my pocket. The Royal Mail office finally offered a berth but in the ship's hospital. At Vigo, lots of the South American passengers disembarked and afterward there was a regular berth in a passenger cabin.'

Des Kirkpatrick returned to his job at the Manchester Ship Canal. 'I used to take walks during lunchtime and after work around the docks. I saw all sorts of ships, coming from all over the world. It was all very fascinating – and rather quickly I thought of going to sea. I wrote to and applied to several shipping lines and Royal Mail Lines was the first to reply. They brought me to London, to their offices along Leadenhall Street, for an interview. I was quickly hired, in April 1956, and assigned to the *Gascony*; a freighter that was the second oldest ship in the fleet. The *Gascony* was on Royal Mail's Caribbean run – from the UK to Bermuda, Nassau, the Dominican Republic and then Kingston, Jamaica. We also called at small Jamaican 'out ports', at places like Falmouth and Montego Bay. We'd anchor out and were loaded with rum and bulk sugar by lighters. The rum came in large barrels, which were loaded four or five at a time. Once, a barrel dropped and smashed on deck and the entire ship smelled of rum.'

Later, Kirkpatrick was assigned to Royal Mail's other freighters, some of which carried up to twelve passengers. 'I sailed on the *Parima*, *Pilcomayo*, *Loch Garth*, *Ebro* and *Paraguay*. I also did several trips on chartered ships, including one flying the Swiss flag, and registered at Basel. Then I was transferred to a more luxurious, more comfortable way of life at sea – to the flagship *Andes* and one of the finest liners of her day.'

The last four of the Highland class soldiered on until the late fifties. The *Highland Monarch*, the eldest, dating from 1928, was thirty-two when she reached the breakers at Dalmuir on 28 April 1960. Months before, in October 1959, the *Highland Chieftain* was sold to Gibraltar-based Calpe Shipping Company. Renamed *Calpean Star*, her passenger-carrying days were over, however – she was now a maintenance and transport vessel for Antarctic whaling fleets. Her new career was quite brief. In March 1960, she had to unexpectedly return from Antarctic waters with rudder damage. She made for Montevideo for repairs. But on 1 June, after putting back to sea, there was an engine room explosion two miles off the Uruguay coast. She was partially sunk and abandoned. The disintegrating remains

Above: A baggage sticker from the Highland ships. (Author's Collection)

Left: The London Docks crammed with ships and with the *Dominion Monarch* and one of the Highland ships in the lower right. (Royal Mail Lines)

SANTOS   BRAZIL

THIRD CLASS

BREAKFAST

Cereals   Oatmeal Porridge
Cod Roes Anglaise
Fried Egg
Grilled Breakfast Bacon
White Bread   Butter   Preserves
Tea   Coffee

LUNCHEON

Potage Bretonne
Vermicelli au Parmesan
Stewed Steak & Onions
Mashed Potatoes
Spring Greens

Third class breakfast menu.
(Des Kirkpatrick Collection)

An atmospheric painting by superb
artist Stephen Card of the outbound
Highland Monarch at London.
(Stephen Card Collection)

were scrapped in 1965. The *Highland Brigade* and *Highland Princess* were sold as a pair to Greek shipowner John S. Latsis. Latsis was involved mainly in the tanker trade, but also dabbled in the carrying of Muslim pilgrims. In this case, he had a new venture in mind: carrying migrants from Genoa to Australia. In preparation, the *Brigade* had a refit – one funnel was removed – but then never entered migrant service. Instead, she was used on seasonal pilgrim voyages to and from Djeddah. Renamed *Henrietta* (the original choice was *Hellos*), she was then promptly renamed *Marianna*, replacing the *Marianna* (ex-*Highland Princess*), which had been sold to Czech buyers. After five years, she was sold to Taiwanese scrappers and arrived at Kaohsiung on 29 June 1965 for demolition. The *Highland Princess* also went to Latsis, was renamed *Marianna*, but then was quickly resold to the Prague-based Czechoslovak Ocean Shipping Company; an intermediary company which renamed her *Slapy*. Rather quickly, however, she was resold to the China Ocean Shipping Company and was renamed *Guanghua*. Based mostly at Shanghai, she was used in coastal passenger service and, on occasion, carrying Chinese workers to and from East Africa. Her exact whereabouts became rather vague by the 1970s, but it has been reported that she was finally scrapped in or about 1988. By then, she would have been about fifty-eight years of age, the last of the Nelson Line and the last surviving passenger ship once owned by Royal Mail Lines.

6. Cruising on the *Atlantis* (ex-*Andes*)

The inviting Smoking Room aboard the all-first-class *Atlantis*. (Norman Knebel Collection)

Refuge at sea: the cosy Winter Garden. (Norman Knebel Collection)

The Main Bar where American-style cocktails were served. Appropriately, it was called the American Bar. (Norman Knebel Collection)

Welcome aboard: the Main Foyer aboard the *Atlantis*. (Norman Knebel Collection)

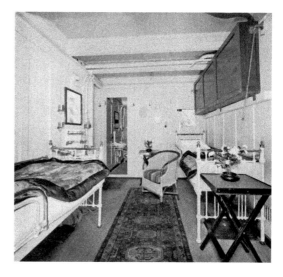

Number 143: a twin-bedded stateroom with private bathroom. (Norman Knebel Collection)

Relaxation at sea: an afternoon game of quoits. (Norman Knebel Collection)

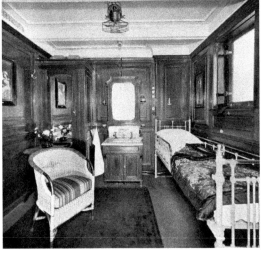

Shipboard comfort: a first class single. (Norman Knebel Collection)

Fun in the sun: swimming on the aft deck. (Norman Knebel Collection)

The bedroom of a first class suite. (Norman Knebel Collection)

Keeping fit: the gymnasium aboard the club-like *Atlantis*. (Norman Knebel Collection)

Exotic ports of call and passengers going ashore. (Norman Knebel Collection)

The fresh sea air: ladies' deck tennis. (Norman Knebel Collection)

Cruising – leisure voyages to 'new and exciting places, and often following the sun' – grew steadily in popularity in the 1920s. Royal Mail Lines found cruising to be interesting, to be an alternative service and to be profitable. They began promoting these voyages that 'escaped the everyday routine'. While the company had offered some cruising in the pre-First World War years, it was in 1923 that it all became more serious and purposeful. Their 'new' *Arcadian* was introduced to full-time cruising.

The *Arcadian* was in fact not new at all. She had been the *Asturias*, built in 1908 for the Southampton–South America run but then torpedoed while serving as a hospital ship on 20 March 1917. Seemingly a total loss, she was then in the hands of the Admiralty. Royal Mail was compensated for her loss, but then, rather strangely, she was bought back and towed to Belfast for full repairs, restoration and conversion to a cruise ship. She was fitted with fresh accommodations, which Royal Mail described as 'having some style'.

Carrying 350 passengers in all-first class configuration, the *Arcadian* cruised from Southampton to the Mediterranean, West Africa, the Atlantic Isles, to the Norwegian fjords and the Baltic cities in summer and occasionally between New York and Bermuda. She was an instant success, drawing repeat passengers and pleasing company accountants. In 1925, her fleetmates *Orbita*, *Orca* and *Ohio* were running occasional cruises as well. The *Orca* tended to cruise between New York and the Caribbean, while the *Ohio* was chartered for voyages to the Mediterranean; especially to Rome for Holy Year pilgrimages. Meanwhile, the *Orca* made the occasional long, luxurious cruise – such as 'The Three Continents' cruise in the winter of 1926. In sixty-five nights, she cruised from Southampton to the Caribbean, then along the East Coast of South America and then over to South and East Africa.

As the South American liner trades slumped somewhat, Royal Mail actually saw better returns in cruising. In 1927, both the *Avon* and *Araguaya* spent considerable time cruising rather than on line voyages. But by 1929–30, the company opted to concentrate their cruise operation in an even more specially outfitted ship, the 15,600 grt *Atlantis*. She would become one of Britain's most popular cruise ships in the years between the wars. Her first cruise was in the summer of 1930.

She too had been reconditioned, having been the 1913-built *Andes* and used on the three-class South American liner trade. Sensibly renamed *Atlantis*, repainted in all white and with all-first accommodations for a rather club-like 450 passengers, she was a very purposeful, very well fitted ship. She had many single cabins, for example, and each was fitted with beds (rather than bunks), electric fans and hot and cold running water. There was a single sitting in the dining room, two verandah cafes and the novelty of an American Bar featuring a new craze: mixed cocktails. There was also a gymnasium, portable swimming pool, lots of open-air deck space, a hair salon as well as barber shop, gift shop, excursion office and well-equipped hospital. Activities included evening dancing on deck (and under the stars), deck games, sunbathing, evening cinema, nightly entertainment and occasional special events: Welcome Aboard Dinner, Carnival Night, Masquerade Ball, Parade of Hats and Pirates Night. Food and service were of very high levels and sometimes appraised as being even greater than first class on the *Asturias* and *Alcantara* on the South American liner run. Happily, by the late 1930s, Royal Mail could boast of more than 50 per cent repeat customers on some *Atlantis* cruises. Her voyages were described as 'cruising at its best', and yet in competition with the likes of Blue Star Line's renowned *Arandora Star* and Cunard's splendid *Carinthia* and *Franconia*. The *Atlantis* was also noted as being very steady – 'a very good sea boat,' commented one of her captains.

Below left: A brochure cover. (Norman Knebel Collection)

Below right: Cruising to romantic destinations. (Norman Knebel Collection)

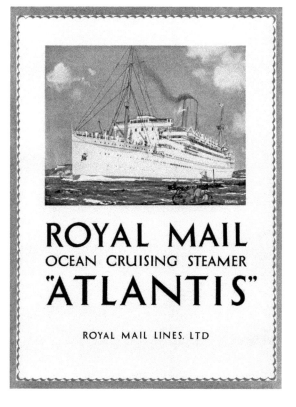

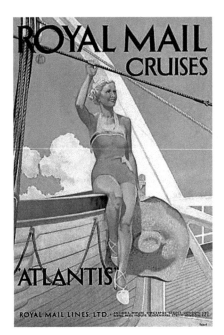 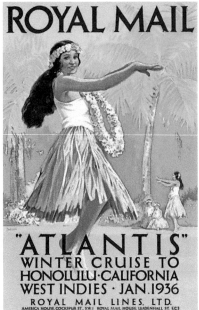

Above left: Happy times at sea! (Norman Knebel Collection)

Above right: Cruising to far-off California and Hawaii from Southampton. (Norman Knebel Collection)

Below left: To the historic Mediterranean in the spring of 1936. (Norman Knebel Collection)

Below right: Autumn cruises. (Norman Knebel Collection)

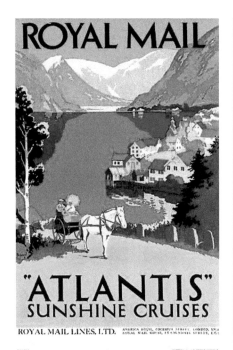

Above left: Once again: more of Norway! (Norman Knebel Collection)

Above right: Cruises to Norway were very popular in the 1930s. (Norman Knebel Collection)

Below left: Artistic style: a classic Royal Mail poster. (Norman Knebel Collection)

Below right: The great appeal of visiting beautiful Venice. (Norman Knebel Collection)

ROYAL
MAIL

"ATLANTIS"
SUNSHINE CRUISES
ROYAL MAIL LINES LTD
AMERICA HOUSE, COCKSPUR STREET, SW1·ROYAL MAIL HOUSE, LEADENHALL STREET, E.C.3

Left: Relaxing times aboard the beautiful *Atlantis*. (Norman Knebel Collection)

Below: Migrant service to Australia: the *Atlantis* in the late 1940s. (Alex Duncan)

A sample cruise program from Southampton for the *Atlantis* in 1935 read:

Feb	Canary Islands, West Africa, Portugal (twenty days)
Mar	Mediterranean (twenty-three days)
Apr	Mediterranean (twenty-three days)
May	Western Mediterranean (nineteen days)
Jun	North Africa and Portugal (fifteen days)
Jul	Northern Capitals (thirteen days)
Jul	Norwegian fjords (seven days)
Aug	Northern Capitals (fifteen days)
Sep	Mediterranean (twenty-one days)
Sep	Mediterranean (eighteen days)
Oct	Mediterranean (seventeen days)
Dec	Canary Islands, Madeira and West Africa (twenty days)

From its London offices, Royal Mail would send out 'cruise post cards' to passengers reminding them of forthcoming voyages. Fares were reasonable such that seven nights to Norway was available from 11 guineas, or approximately £12 in 2016 currency.

Occasionally, the *Atlantis* would also make longer, more luxurious cruises – such as to the West Indies, South America, the Pacific and Indian oceans and to ports in the USA. Business grew such that both the *Asturias* and *Alcantara* would take breaks from their three-class South American sailings and offer cruises. In January 1935, for example, the *Asturias* set off from Southampton on a sixty-five-day cruise through the Mediterranean and Suez, then to Ceylon, the Straits Settlements, the East Indies and then home via South and West Africa. Fares began at 145 guineas.

But dramatic times were ahead. When war clouds were quickly forming, in August 1939, the *Atlantis* stopped cruising and was called to duty. Royal Mail would not resume cruising until the 1950s, but then only occasionally and then full-time again in 1960 with the refitted *Andes*.

Especially for its *Atlantis* cruising in the 1930s, Royal Mail used the great talents of commercial artist Kenneth Shoesmith. With a unique style of recreating the ships, shipboard life and especially the ports of call, Shoesmith created some of the most evocative, colourful and cherished travel artwork of his time. He prepared posters, menu cards, calendars, playing cards, booklets, blotters and a splendid array of post cards. His work remains highly collectible to this day. After his death, at age forty-eight in 1939, his ashes were scattered at sea, quite appropriately, from the *Asturias*.

The *Atlantis* herself, despite having been sold to the British Government in September 1939, remained under Royal Mail Lines management. After service as a hospital ship and then trooper, she was rebuilt as a migrant ship – with 900 all-third class berths – in 1948. She was scrapped in 1952.

7. The Luxurious *Andes*

These days, Royal Mail is long gone; first having been more fully integrated into Britain's Furness Withy shipping group, which was later sold off to the Chinese and then to the Germans. Most recently, Furness Withy's remaining shipping interests were a part of mighty Hamburg-Sud – the Hamburg-South American Line, a onetime competitor.

In its twilight, in 1969, Royal Mail's *Amazon* and her two sisters were sold off, going to the Shaw Savill Line but for a very short, very unsuccessful time (Shaw Savill was also part of the Furness Withy family) before being sold and totally rebuilt for the Norwegians as bulky auto-carriers. They were the last passenger links to the once-staple UK–South America trade. But, in fact, the grand old *Andes* proved to be the last of the Royal Mail passenger liners. She ran her final cruise out of Southampton in April 1971, and then made a short hop across the Channel to Belgium, where she was broken up. Later, as a reminder of those stylish ocean liner days, Royal Mail operated a containership on the UK–South America run. Sentimentally, she was named *Andes*.

A superb view of the beautiful *Andes* at Cherbourg. (Anton Logvinenko Collection)

Above: Another view at Cherbourg: the *Andes* departing with the *Queen Mary* behind. (Author's Collection)

Right: Arrival: the *Andes* at Santos. (Author's Collection)

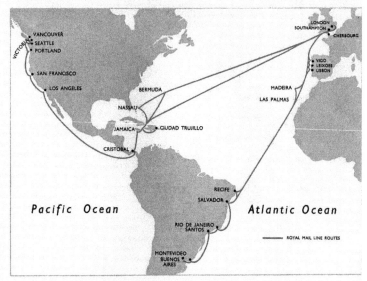

Royal Mail Lines' services in the 1950s. (Des Kirkpatrick Collection)

The completion of the 25,689 grt *Andes* in September 1939 was marked not simply as the completion of Royal Mail Lines' largest and most luxurious passenger ship built to date, but signified the centenary of the firm itself. It had been exactly 100 years since a royal charter had been granted to the company that became the Royal Mail Steam Packet Company. Consequently, the arrival of the new flagship *Andes* was more than just another new passenger liner. Yet, despite all the joyous and detailed planning, the outbreak of hostilities – with Britain declaring war on Nazi Germany on 3 September 1939 – changed everything. The war started in earnest just three weeks before the new vessel's departure from Southampton to South America on her flag-bedecked, party-filled maiden voyage.

The 669-foot-long ship was launched on 7 March 1939, by the Viscountess Craigavon – the wife of the Prime Minister of Northern Ireland – at the Harland & Wolff yard at Belfast. Princess Marina, the popular Duchess of Kent and wife of Prince George (a son of George V and Queen Mary) was to have done the honours, but political uncertainty in Northern Ireland at the time made a royal visit both uncertain and inappropriate.

Meticulous care had been taken in the new ship's design and decoration so that she would not only be Royal Mail's finest liner yet, but a sure competitor to the high standard French, Italian and German liners already in service to the South Atlantic, to the east coast of South America. The French, as an example, were adding the finishing touches to the 29,200 grt *Pasteur*, which was to join the Compagnie Sud Atlantique's service to South

America, also in September 1939. Further consideration had been given to cruising – long, luxurious cruises – for the *Andes* and so she was fitted with a large bunker capacity.

The *Andes* was still at the fitting-out dock at Belfast when war was declared and promptly her maiden departure from Southampton – set for 26 September – was cancelled. The supplies and deliveries of handsome, high-standard fittings were set aside and re-routed to storage in warehouses. The freshly painted hull, superstructure and yellow funnel were redone in sombre shades of grey. The gala send-off, the festivities, the capacity list of inaugural passengers and the maiden calls at South American ports suddenly seemed inappropriate and far less important. The more detailed career of the *Andes* in the Second World War is in Chapter 8.

The *Andes* returned to Belfast in 1947 for conversion to a commercial liner; to a standard which was even more modern as well as comfortable than had been intended in 1939. When she left Southampton on her long-delayed maiden voyage to South America on 22 January 1948, she was – as a result of wartime casualties – both the largest and finest liner serving the South Atlantic. At high speed, she could travel from Southampton to Buenos Aires via

Above left: Bound for Rio: an alluring night-time view. (Norman Knebel Collection)

Above right: In poster art, the liners are often made to appear very large. (Norman Knebel Collection)

R.M.S. "Andes"—Flagship—Royal Mail Lines Ltd. Built by Harland & Wolff Ltd., Belfast. Weight, 25,676 tons; Length, 669½ ft.; Breadth, 83½ ft.; Depth, 47½ ft.; Service speed, 21 knots. Passengers, 324 first class, 204 second class. Twin-screw turbines, U.K./S. America service.

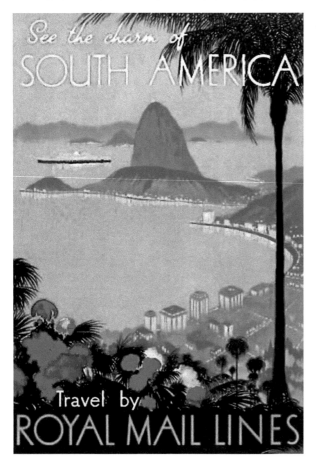

Above: A cigarette card view of the beautiful *Andes*. (Author's Collection)

Left: Faraway shores: the beauty of Rio de Janeiro and its harbour. (Norman Knebel Collection)

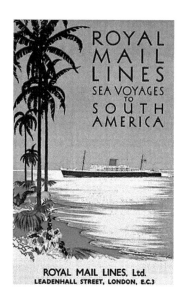

Alternates: sailings from London or Southampton. (Norman Knebel Collection)

Brochure cover for the *Andes* dated 1955. (Des Kirkpatrick Collection)

Drinks before dinner: the Cocktail Bar. (Royal Mail Lines)

A comfortable double-bedded stateroom. (Royal Mail Lines)

The imposing Grand Hall in the 1950s. (Des Kirkpatrick Collection)

Welcoming and comfortable: the First Class Smoking Room. (Des Kirkpatrick Collection)

FIRST CLASS LIDO COCKTAIL LOUNGE

Another view of the Cocktail Bar. (Des Kirkpatrick Collection)

FIRST CLASS FOYER

Welcoming passengers: the ship's Main Foyer. (Des Kirkpatrick Collection)

FIRST CLASS DINING SALOON

The superb First Class Dining Room. (Des Kirkpatrick Collection)

The sitting room of a suite aboard the *Andes*. (Des Kirkpatrick Collection)

SUITE DE LUXE BEDROOM

Colourful decor: the bedroom of a suite. (Des Kirkpatrick Collection)

FIRST CLASS BED SITTING ROOM

A single with adjoining
sitting room. (Des Kirkpatrick
Collection)

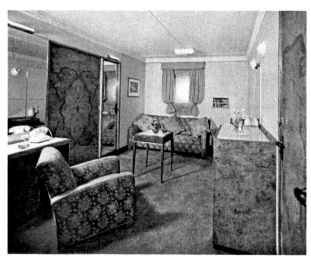

FIRST CLASS BED SITTING ROOM WITH BED CONCEALED

The same single but with the
bed concealed. (Des Kirkpatrick
Collection)

FIRST CLASS DOUBLE ROOM

A spacious first class double.
(Des Kirkpatrick Collection)

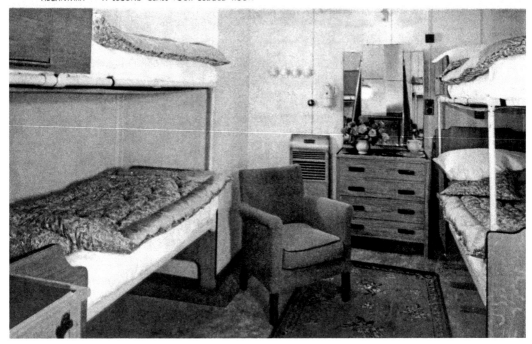

A four-berth cabin in second class. (Des Kirkpatrick Collection)

Cherbourg, Lisbon, Las Palmas, Rio de Janeiro, Santos and Montevideo in sixteen days. Her berthing arrangements were modified and now balanced between 324 in high-standard first class and 204 in more moderate, but still comfortable second class. There was no provision for a third class, for immigrants mostly from Spain and Portugal, which were instead handled by Royal Mail's smaller Highland class of liners. Aboard the *Andes*, every cabin was outside and the first class berthing included four deluxe suites as well as several cabins with a bed/sitting room arrangement. Along with beautifully furnished public rooms, there was an outdoor pool and sunning area on deck, a theatre for late afternoon as well as evening performances and, at a slightly later date, air-conditioning in the main restaurant and foyer.

Southern waters: 'My father had business in Argentina. He was in management and so had extended travel privileges,' remembered a lady from Falmouth in England. 'We were sent out to Buenos Aires for two years in the late 1950s. We sailed out on the *Andes* in first class and which was very grand. It was all very gracious British service – grand afternoon teas, long and very formal dinners and lots of dressing. There were some wealthy passengers onboard including some very rich Argentines, who travelled with their personal servants. It took about two weeks from Southampton to Buenos Aires. We returned to London on the *Uruguay Star*, but which was a very different ship. It carried only fifty passengers and, compared to the *Andes*, was very quiet, less formal. But both ships were very memorable experiences. I hadn't thought of them in years, but your lectures on liners [onboard the *Queen Mary 2*] brought back many, many memories.'

The South American liner trade began to decline, however, by the mid-1950s for British-flag liners such as the *Andes*. Aside from normal South American service, to which she was teamed with another pre-war liner, the *Alcantara*, the *Andes* was given over to periodic cruising for at least several weeks each year. Her speciality became millionaire-style long-distance voyages that took her through the Mediterranean, to Scandinavia in summer and then further afield to South Africa, the Caribbean, California via Panama, to Port Everglades and New Orleans – and on one occasion to New York via Bermuda. She visited in July 1959, arriving the very same week as the newly rebuilt West German flagship *Bremen*. The *Andes* berthed at Pier 97, at the foot of West 57th Street, remained there for three days and was looked after by the Furness-Bermuda Line. But possibly one of her most unique cruises was in fact a short one – a mini-cruise from Southampton along the southern coast, but acting as a luxury spectator vessel at Queen Elizabeth II's Coronation Review in June 1953. She was one of the largest of the 160 ships present in a fleet that stretched all the way to Cowes.

The *Andes* finally closed out the long-established South American service from Southampton in November 1959. Alternately, Royal Mail's three brand new *Amazon* class sisters would be based at London. The flagship – having reached two-thirds of her expected life – was sent to the De Schelde shipyard in Vlissingen, Holland, for a major refit. Hereafter, with her accommodation for 480 all-first class passengers, the *Andes* would be used for year-round cruising. The refit itself was rather unusual, being done in two stages with a forty-six-night cruise to the Caribbean and Florida in between. When she departed on her first official cruise, on 10 June 1960, it was noted that she was Britain's first full-time cruise ship since 1939. Cunard's larger *Caronia*, while primarily used for cruising, still made occasional two-class transatlantic crossings. While the *Caronia* was aimed at the upper-market in cruising in America, the *Andes* was soon said to be her British-based equivalent. Quickly, the *Andes* secured a position as one of the finest cruise ships ever to sail and had a character and ambience that was akin to a posh sea-going club.

After serving on Royal Mail freighters, Des Kirkpatrick joined the *Andes* as assistant purser in June 1960. He would sail that ship for the next eighteen months. 'She was an elegant, nicely appointed ship highlighted by tremendous deck space. There were very pleasant public rooms, a dining room, grill room and a theatre. Umbrellas surrounded the outdoor pool. The cabins were very 1930s and all of them with private facilities. There was no 'down the corridor' on the Andes. We usually carried about 400 passengers. We would bring local entertainment onboard in the ports of call, but carried a dance band, a dance couple and sometimes a vocalist and a conjuror. There was also a bridge lecturer and port lecturer. The officers tended to stick together by department, but dined together in the officers' mess. The captain was a classic, old fashioned ship's master.'

'The passengers were all British and almost all upper class,' added Des Kirkpatrick. 'The *Andes* was very, very British – afternoon tea, long dinners and a quiet but well-run tone. She catered to the upper classes, to titled people and chiefs of business. There was a very high number of repeaters, often over 75%. There were also some elderly widows and spinsters. Deck sports were very popular during the day and then there was dining, dancing and some light entertainment in the evening. There was a cruise director, a social hostess and a skilled tour department from Thomas Cook. There were two big tenders, nested on the

Cruising aboard the *Andes* in the 1960s. (Author's Collection)

Sunny waters: off duty with Royal Mail.
(Des Kirkpatrick Collection)

The *Andes* was often
said to look like a big,
white yacht. (Michael
D. J. Lennon)

Night-time at Madeira: the *Andes* on the left, the *Reina Del Mar* to the right. (Author's Collection)

Classic lines: the *Andes* at Southampton. (David Williams Collection)

Andes cruising in 1964. (Author's Collection)

CRUISE No. 5   **22 days**

PORT	Miles	ARRIVE	DEPART	Hours in Port
SOUTHAMPTON			Thursday 2nd JULY 12.45 p.m.	
TRONDHEIM	1001	Sunday 5th JULY Noon	Sunday 5th JULY 7 p.m.	7
NORTH CAPE	635	Tuesday 7th JULY 7 p.m.	Wednesday 8th JULY 1 a.m.	6
TROMSO	175	Wednesday 8th JULY Noon	Wednesday 8th JULY 6 p.m.	6
SVOLVAER	185	Thursday 9th JULY 6 a.m.	Thursday 9th JULY 2 p.m.	8
YTTERDAL	456	Saturday 11th JULY 8 a.m.	Saturday 11th JULY 10 a.m.	2
MEROK	22	Saturday 11th JULY Noon	Saturday 11th JULY 6 p.m.	6
OSLO	574	Monday 13th JULY 6 a.m.	Monday 13th JULY 6 p.m.	12
COPENHAGEN	272	Tuesday 14th JULY 2 p.m.	Thursday 16th JULY 4 p.m.	50
STOCKHOLM	650	Saturday 18th JULY 8 a.m.	Saturday 18th JULY 6 p.m.	10
KIEL CANAL	504	Monday 20th JULY	Transit daylight	
HAMBURG	95	Monday 20th JULY 11 p.m.	Wednesday 22nd JULY 11 p.m.	48
SOUTHAMPTON	568	Friday 24th JULY 8 a.m.		

Above: Summer cruising to Norway and the Fjords. (Author's Collection)

Left: The *Andes* anchored off the famed French Riviera. (Author's Collection)

foredeck, that were very good for use in the smaller cruise ports. They were actually quite big, carrying up to 100 each.'

The style of the cruising *Andes* was a great reminder of a bygone era in sea travel. Some of her passengers even remembered the era of another company cruise ship – the *Atlantis*, in the 1930s. John Draffin served in the Purser's Department aboard the *Andes* in the ship's final decade, in the 1960s. He remembered, 'She was an exceptionally elegant ship, a vessel of the old style and old school. Sailing day at Southampton was like the first day back at school, but a posh public school. Almost all the passengers were 'regulars' and therefore knew one another. The Who's Who of Britain would be aboard. Passengers in the best suites brought along their own servants. There were, of course, more crew members than needed, but then that was the standard Royal Mail preferred. There were special facilities and considerations for older passengers. On some voyages, we had more wheelchairs aboard than many hospitals. While we always carried a full dance band, the demand was, in fact, for very limited entertainment. Ironically, in later years, in the second half of the Sixties, our biggest competitor was the *Reina Del Mar*, which was basically a tourist-class-style cruise ship that sailed for Union-Castle, but which was actually owned by Pacific Steam Navigation – a division of the Furness Withy Group, which also owned Royal Mail. However, while the *Reina Del Mar* catered to corporate Britain, the *Andes* carried aristocratic Britain.'

The late Bob Cummins served in the Stewards' Department onboard the *Andes* and also in the Sixties. He recalled, 'The *Andes* was an exceptionally beautiful liner that was in the highest class, possibly even more so than some of the famed Cunarders, with the rather obvious exception of the legendary *Caronia*. The *Andes* was actually a floating clubhouse, filled with gentry and millionaires, who met two or three times a year onboard. With about 400 passengers served and looked after by an equal number of staff, we had a select one-to-one service ratio. It was all very English: mid-morning bouillon, ritual afternoon tea, formal dinners at one sitting. As stewards, we had to don formal dinner suits and our response to almost any request was either 'Yes, Madam' or 'Yes, Sir'.'

On 13 October 1962, the *Andes* had to be placed in the King George V Graving Dock at Southampton unexpectedly. It seems she had lost one of her propellers when entering Lisbon harbour just weeks before while on a Mediterranean cruise. Captain Peterson, master of the liner, described the loss as a 'profound mystery'.

In 1967, the *Andes* was reconditioned and modernized – again in two stages – in May–June and in December. Her Christmas–New Year cruise had to be cancelled. Her boilers were re-tubed, which supposedly guaranteed she would last well into the early 1970s. But apart from aging, the *Andes* was facing another problem: gradually declining passenger loads. The old millionaire crowd, that aristocratic set of followers, was dying off.

Soon after her reconditioning, in January 1968, the *Andes* set off on her longest cruise yet, a 25,000-mile voyage from Southampton to the Far East and which included stops at Hong Kong, Manila and Singapore. Soon afterward, Royal Mail announced that in her eight years as a fulltime cruise ship, the *Andes* had carried 40,000 passengers and steamed over 600,000 miles. Altogether, she had made ninety cruises. It was also noted that 60 per cent of her passengers were repeat customers. Later that same year, in August, the ship carried its 65,000th cruise passenger.

According to John Draffin, 'The *Andes* was becoming increasingly more expensive, especially after the devastating British Seamen's Strike in the spring of 1966, which lasted six weeks and cost some £4 million. Unfortunately, her problems were compounded as she began sailing with fewer and fewer passengers – sometimes as few as 200 on some voyages. Royal Mail brought in some rather brash, flashy entertainment in an effort to recruit new, preferably younger passengers, but which instead managed to alienate the remaining, older, loyalist ones. The Furness Withy Group, having just closed out its Furness-Bermuda Line operations at New York [November 1966], thought of building two new 20,000-ton cruise ships, one of which would replace the *Andes*. Having all the contemporary amenities and intended to be based mostly in the Caribbean, they were intended to be quite innovative as 'bed and breakfast' ships. The cabin accommodation would be included in the fares, but there would be additional, quite separate charges for the onboard restaurants. Alternately, passengers would have the option of dining ashore. Also, there were ideas of converting one of the *Amazon* sisters into a cruise ship or rebuilding a large freighter with passenger accommodations. However, the final decision was that Furness Withy, and therefore Royal Mail, saw container ships and bulk carriers as far better investments. The days of Royal Mail Lines's passenger shipping were clearly numbered as far as they were concerned.'

Ardent cruise traveller Gordon Dalzell added, 'The *Andes* was immaculate, had an old world atmosphere and was run with a club-like atmosphere. In all white, she even looked like a big, luxurious yacht. There were two large launches especially for port calls, one of which was used often by a very rich passenger and therefore known as his 'private chariot'. But in her last seasons, the *Andes* had past her best: the pipes were bursting, the air-conditioning would break down and there would be plumbing problems. But most of the passengers were deep loyalists and accepted these problems and discomforts. I don't think the *Andes* was a spectacular vessel, just a good, old-fashioned, solid ship.'

When Royal Mail began evaluating plans for a replacement in the mid-1960s, the outcome was also greatly discoloured by the extreme rise in shipbuilding costs and even by the high costs of, say, converting a suitable second-hand liner. Operating costs under the British flag were another decisive consideration and the greatly disruptive six-week British seamen's strike in May–June 1966 probably dealt the final blow. It was finally decided, with some regret, for Royal Mail to abandon passenger services altogether. The *Andes* was finally decommissioned in the spring of 1971. The two final cruises were also among the ship's most diverse. She departed from Southampton on 10 January on a forty-day sailing that called at Las Palmas, Luanda, Durban, Cape Town, Dakar and Lisbon. This was followed, on 20 February, by a nostalgic thirty-nine-night cruise to Lisbon, Tenerife, Rio de Janeiro, Recife, Trinidad, Curaçao and Madeira. Afterward, she was quickly sold to Belgian shipbreakers Van Heyghen Freres, and delivered at Ghent on 7 May. Just before, there was a tearful send-off from Southampton. In the hands of a small caretaker crew, she even looked particularly sad: her twin masts had been stumped for bridge clearance in Belgium.

Sentimental voyage: the *Andes* departs from Southampton bound for the breakers in Belgium. (Southern Newspapers Ltd)

ROYAL MAIL LINES

CARGO/PASSENGER LINERS TO
NORTH PACIFIC COAST
VIA WEST INDIES & CENTRAL AMERICA

Royal Mail carried up to twelve passengers aboard its freighters, such as the *Loch Gowan*. (Des Kirkpatrick Collection)

Spacious accommodation aboard the *Loch Gowan*. (Des Kirkpatrick Collection)

Twelve-passenger comfort: the forward-facing lounge. (Des Kirkpatrick Collection)

" Loch Gowan "— Dining Saloon

Officers joined the twelve passengers for meals on these Royal Mail freighters. (Des Kirkpatrick Collection)

8. Royal Mail Liners Go to War

Britain declared war on Nazi Germany on 3 September 1939. Immediately, everything – including operations on worldwide sea lanes – changed. British shipowners hurriedly scrambled to assist the Government and prepare to have any and all ships requisitioned and 'called to duty'. Shipping lines also worried – and often very seriously – about the safety on the seas. British ships were hereafter open targets. Even as early as the winter of 1938, British ships were being prepared in what was termed 'the uneasy political situation in Europe'. Crews on the passenger ships in particular were given added training in the likes of damage control, ship rescue and fire extinguishing. Two months before war was actually declared, in July 1939, Royal Mail passenger ships were specially carrying buckets of grey paint, gas masks, sand and so-called blue lamps. By mid-August, Government instructions were for ships to take on extra supplies and especially extra foodstuffs. Even before the

The troopship *Andes* departing from Southampton in 1945. (Royal Mail Lines)

Offloading military passengers. (Royal Mail Lines)

Sleeping on deck during a steamy transit of the Suez Canal. (Royal Mail Lines)

Lining the decks: visit to Port Said in 1945. (Royal Mail Lines)

The *Asturias* – but with her funnel repainted in Royal Mail buff-yellow – at Southampton in 1946. (Anton Logvinenko)

actual declaration, ships began to sail blacked-out at night and requested that passengers help during the day to repaint areas of the vessel in grey.

The aged *Almanzora* – arriving at Southampton after a very tense northbound voyage from South America – was among the first of the company liners to be requisitioned, on 8 September. She and her fleetmates would be called to serve as troopships, armed merchant cruisers and hospital ships. The years ahead would be dramatic, tense, disruptive and often destructive. In the autumn of 1939, Royal Mail had thirty-one ships in its fleet, altogether amounting to 300,000 gross tons; by 1945, twenty-one of them had been sunk. Over 200 souls aboard Royal Mail ships were lost during the war.

The sailing patterns of the Royal Mail passenger ships were expectedly diverse. The *Almanzora* crossed to Canada and then to North and South Africa, India and the Suez. In 1944, hard-pressed but steaming on, she helped with the Allied landings on Sicily and then later delivered re-occupation forces in Malaya. Even after the war ended in August 1945, she was still very active. That September, she carried a full load of prisoners and internees from Japanese-occupied Southeast Asia back from Britain. Then it was off to repatriation service – with more prisoners as well as refugees -- from various European ports. All but exhausted, the thirty-two-year-old *Almanzora* was decommissioned in 1947 and scrapped a year later.

The brand new *Andes* was to sail from Southampton on her gala maiden voyage to South America on 26 September. Her delivery and maiden voyage was to mark the centenary of the Royal Mail Lines. That never happened and instead her first voyage, now under the jurisdiction of the Ministry of War Transport, took her from England on 9 December to Halifax. There were no celebrations, no strings of colourful flags and gala welcomes to port and certainly no full load of happy passengers. Her intended 600 passengers as guests, in ocean-going comfort, were replaced by a capacity of as many as 4,000 troops, often in crowded, cramped quarters. The liner was now also in grey war paint; drab and attempting to be less recognisable. From Halifax, the *Andes* returned with the first load of Canadian troops brought to Britain for the war effort. From there, the 21-knot, steam-turbine-driven liner-troopship set a course through the Mediterranean, passed through the Suez Canal, stopped at Colombo and then Singapore, and finally reached Hong Kong. She had reached an area of the world far removed from any of her original intentions and design. Quickly, she was ordered south to Lyttleton and Wellington, and then dispatched homeward again through the Indian Ocean. She was, during this trip, one of a large and mighty convoy that included the *Queen Mary, Aquitania, Mauretania, Empress of Britain, Empress of Japan* and *Empress of Canada*. Despite the sadness and urgency of the time, what an incredible sight these seven liners, even while painted entirely in grey, must have made to passing ships. Altogether, there was a total of nineteen funnels!

The following voyages for the *Andes* included a roundtrip to Iceland, and then a sailing to the Middle East, but now via the South African Cape. On that voyage, she had 3,000 servicemen aboard and was so overcrowded that 500 of them slept on deck and so international that thirteen different languages were spoken. Thereafter, her voyages were extremely diverse and included visits to ports throughout the world. It has been recorded, however, that she again featured in one of the world's great convoys; this one including Cunard-White Star's *Georgic*, several P&O 'Strath' liners, an equal number of Canadian Pacific Empress and Duchess ships, at least a pair of Orient Line's 'O Boats', various Castles from Union Castle, the French *Pasteur* and the Dutch *Dempo* and *Johan van Oldenbarnevelt.*

In 1942, the valiant *Andes* steamed completely around the world in eighty days – sailing via the South African Cape, Colombo, Melbourne, the Panama Canal, Boston and Halifax before returning to the UK. On that voyage, she had steamed some 38,000 miles and altogether carried over 14,500 troops. Later in the War she was used on the North Atlantic; ferrying American and Canadian soldiers to British ports for the eventual invasion and Allied occupation of Europe.

'In the spring of 1945, I returned home [from Egypt] as a soldier in the British Army. I was aboard the troopship *Andes*,' said Colonel Norman Dodd. 'As a trooper, it was far from her luxury days. We slept five bunks high in the former ballroom. We'd climb up the bunks on cases. There were all kinds of service personnel onboard. There were no diversions during the long voyage home to Liverpool. We had long days at sea. We'd just sit around being scared. Even though the European peace was declared during our voyage, there were frantic rumours that there were some Nazi subs still about, going mad and sinking ships carelessly!'

One of the more glorious duties for the *Andes* during wartime came at the end of hostilities. In May 1945, she was selected to carry the Norwegian government from wartime exile in London across the North Sea to a triumphant reception in liberated Oslo. Aircraft flew overhead, dozens of small craft created an escort and thousands lined the waterfront as the flag-bedecked *Andes* steamed into the capital city. The sounds of horns and sirens filled the air. When the excitement abated, the *Andes* quietly returned to sea for further military duties: repatriation of troops, carrying prisoners of war and transporting the wounded.

On 29 June, the hard-worked *Andes* was off on another long, extended voyage. She departed Liverpool with over 4,000 returning Australian and New Zealand troops. She sailed outbound via the Panama Canal. From Australia, she returned to Southampton via Bombay and the Suez Canal. After reaching Southampton on 10 September, she established a record – a 26,000 mile around-the-world voyage in seventy-two and a half days. The ship's average speed: 15 knots. But there was little time for rest or full repairs – on 24 September, she departed Southampton with 3,500 Australian and New Zealand Air Force officers. Again, it was a fast voyage – Southampton to Melbourne in twenty-three days.

The *Andes* returned to Belfast in 1947 for conversion to a commercial liner, to a standard which was even more modern as well as comfortable than had been intended in 1939.

Both the *Asturias* and *Alcantara* were quickly called to war duties. Days before the war officially began, the *Asturias* was requisitioned, on 29 August, and quickly stripped of her passenger fittings at Southampton. The ship had returned from a Mediterranean cruise just three days before. But times were changing – and changing quickly. The *Alcantara* quickly followed in early September. She was stripped out and then was sent off to the Royal Navy dockyard on Malta and refitted – with eight 6-inch guns – as an armed merchant cruiser. Both ships were changed considerably – most notably, their forward funnels were removed (and never replaced).

The *Alcantara* was dispatched to the South Atlantic, serving as an escort to convoys and on patrols. She saw action, on 28 July 1940, when she encountered the German raider *Thor*. The German vessel was damaged and then fled; the *Alcantara* herself suffered damages. A hole in her side was plugged with rolled-up hammocks while oil was pumped to her port side tanks, which created a significant list and lifted the ship clear of the sea water. Fortunately, the *Alcantara* made it to Rio for repairs. Afterward, she continued as an auxiliary cruiser until 1943, when it was decided that the ship was better suited as a troopship with a capacity of 3–4,000. Duties took her to North Atlantic service, the Mediterranean and out to the Far East.

The *Asturias* spent less time as an escort when, in 1942, she was converted in an American shipyard with more extensive equipment; namely new guns and an aircraft catapult and hangar. In the process, her mainmast was removed and never returned. Her wartime duties were rather short lived, however – in July 1943, the ship was torpedoed about 500 miles off West Africa. She was escorting a slow-moving floating dry dock at the time. Through the extra efforts of her crew through pumping, the flooding was contained and the damaged ship towed to Freetown. In the mixed priorities of war, she remained there for eighteen months. Early in 1945, with the war nearing its end, she was pumped out and afterward towed to Gibraltar and patched up. In June, she was towed to Belfast for full repairs and refitting. Having been officially declared a 'constructive total loss', she remained in the hands of the British Government, but under Royal Mail management. She would never return to luxury passenger service, but see service instead as a peacetime troop ship and to carry low-fare migrants to Australia.

After returning from a Baltic cruise on 25 August 1939, the cruise ship *Atlantis* was called to duty. She was hurriedly converted to *Hospital Ship No. 33*, with wards and related facilities for up to 400 patients. Care was provided by 130 medical staff. The *Atlantis* was repainted with large red crosses along her sides and a wide green band around her hull. She was specially illuminated at night. In all, she too was a heroic, important ship – tending to 35,600 injured while steaming some 280,000 miles.

In the autumn of 1939 and through the winter into 1940, the five Highland sister ships were left on the UK–South America run. They had an important task: bringing much-needed meat from Argentina to Britain. Often, the Highland ships carried over 5,000 tons of refrigerated meat per northbound sailing.

The *Highland Patriot* was a casualty, however. On 1 October 1940, she was homeward bound from Buenos Aires when torpedoed off the Irish coast. Three were lost but 169 passengers and crew survived, being rescued by HMS *Wellington*. At 14,100 gross tons, the *Highland Patriot* would be the largest Royal Mail Line ship to be lost in the Second World War.

By the end of 1940, the remaining four Highland ships began diverse wartime assignments, mostly as troopships. While much of their cargo spaces were converted to troop accommodation, some cargo spaces remained and, on occasion, the ships still carried beef northbound from Argentina. They also delivered consignments of meat to the UK from New Zealand, as well as fruits from Australia, New Zealand and South Africa. In 1943–44, in preparation for the planned invasion of Normandy, these four Highland ships were often used on the North Atlantic, sometimes from New York and delivering American GIs to British ports. At war's end, in 1945, this Highland quartet was assigned to Far East, Southeast Asian and Australian military sailings. They returned troops to Australia, were involved in the re-occupation of Malaya and Burma and repatriated troops and evacuees. The *Highland Brigade* was alone in having a close call. In January 1946, she was damaged by an unmarked mine off Singapore. She had to spend ten weeks in dry dock before returning to the UK.

9. Ship of Misfortune: *Magdalena*

The splendid-looking but ill-fated *Magdalena* during her trials. (Royal Mail Lines)

Preparing her maiden voyage, the *Magdalena* loading in the London Docks. (Royal Mail Lines)

The aft section is lashed by the seas. (Author's Collection)

The forward end is low at the aft end. (Author's Collection)

80

Tragic sight: the remaining two-thirds of the *Magdalena.* (Author's Collection)

A sad view from shoreside. (Author's Collection)

The two sections of the *Magdalena*. (Author's Collection)

Another view from shore. (Author's Collection)

When she set off on her maiden voyage from London to South America in March 1949, the *Magdalena* was noted as one of Britain's most modern passenger ships. She was a one-off; specially built to replace the *Highland Patriot*, which was lost in the war, and to join the remaining Highland liners. She was topped by an all-yellow, pear-shaped funnel. All of her deck structures were rounded, both for appearance and to minimize air resistance, and was consequently dubbed 'the ship of curves'.

At 17,500 gross tons, the *Magdalena* was considered a 'big post-war order' for Harland & Wolff. The ship was launched on 11 May 1948 and delivered in the following February. The fates are strange, however; she would become one of three ships built by Harland & Wolff that sank on its maiden voyage. Obviously, the *Titanic*, which sank on 15 April 1912, is the most famous.

The *Magdalena* might have had a long, productive life, but her time was cut short – very short. On her return maiden voyage from Buenos Aires to London on 25 April, the 570-foot-long ship went aground near the Tijuca Islands; about six miles off the Brazilian coast and about twenty miles south of Rio de Janeiro. An SOS immediately went out. Passengers were quickly evacuated and moved to Brazilian naval vessels. After a night's battering, the all-but-empty ship was re-floated and a careful tow to Rio was arranged. The *Magdalena* rolled heavily, however, and made slow progress. But more troubles were ahead. When almost opposite Sugarloaf Mountain, a roaring noise erupted as the ship suddenly broke in two. The tow rope was promptly severed, the bow rose upward and the ship was abandoned. Her stern was soon firmly aground at the entrance to Guanabara Bay. Passenger baggage and mail were retrieved. Early estimates suggested that the stern section could not be salvaged and saved; the bow section sank within five days, on 30 April.

The gleaming new ship was a complete loss. The work of salvaging her valuable cargo of 2,500 tons of Argentine frozen meats, and 20,000 cases of Brazilian oranges, began on 6 May. The loss of the ship was said to be worth over $10 million.

Bill Harkness organized a small sixtieth reunion in the winter of 2016 of fellow crew members from the *Magdalena*, and her tragic maiden voyage. Some came from far distances, including Australia. Harkness recalled the fateful night: 'I had one leg in my pyjamas and one leg out, balanced in my cabin, when the ship struck. The second time I got the big crunch. It was so severe it threw me against my bunk.' Another reunion member was Charlie Warmington, who recalled, 'We all survived the wreck. No one actually went down with the ship because initially it didn't go down. She crashed onto rocks!' Another former crewman, Reuben Griffiths, added, 'As we were rowing away from the stricken vessel, we heard the creaking and then the cracking – and saw the ship as it broke in half. We finished up landing ourselves on Copacabana Beach – everybody's dream spot, but not landing in a lifeboat!'

10. 'The Three Graces' – *Amazon, Aragon* and *Arlanza* (1960)

The post-Second World War South American passenger service was usually divided between a deluxe, demanding first class market, who wanted nothing but the best in accommodation and in service; if not just for one-way travel, then for roundtrip cruise-like voyages. Then there was a comparatively undemanding market in tourist and third class. Mostly, these passengers travelled southbound, to new lives and employment on the South American continent. Aboard passenger ships coming out of northern waters, the greatest numbers of third class passengers would board at specially arranged calls in Spain and Portugal. Homebound, these same lower deck quarters were often quite empty by the Sixties, filled possibly only with some tourists and students.

Building the new *Amazon* trio in 1959. (Author's Collection)

Above: Between voyages: the *Amazon* in the London Docks. (Tim Noble Collection)

Right: South to Latin America. (Author's Collection)

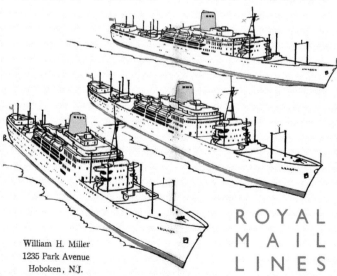

AMAZON
ARAGON
ARLANZA
TO
SOUTH AMERICA
FIRST CLASS

AMAZON
ARAGON
ARLANZA
TO
SOUTH AMERICA
FIRST CLASS

William H. Miller
1235 Park Avenue
Hoboken, N.J.

ROYAL
MAIL
LINES

85

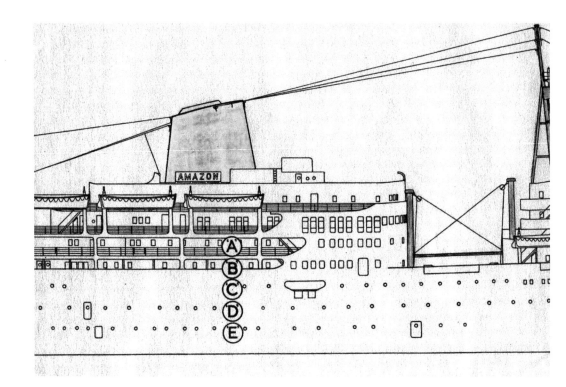

The *Amazon* and her sisters were the last three-class British passenger ships. (Andrew Kilk Collection)

The inviting First Class Smoking Room. (Author's Collection)

The First Class Lido and Pool area. (Author's Collection)

A comfortable first class double-bedded stateroom. (Author's Collection)

The attractive First Class Restaurant. (Author's Collection)

The Cabin
Class Smoking
Room. (Author's
Collection)

The First Class Library-Writing Room. (Author's Collection)

Royal Mail's South American liner service continued for another decade – until 1968–69 – but by then had been entrusted to a brand new trio of handsome-looking passenger-cargo liners; the 20,000-ton *Amazon* and her twin sisters *Aragon* and *Arlanza*. Capped by single, buff-yellow colored funnels, they were in fact the last passenger ships in the British fleet to have 'split' superstructures (the officers being separated from the passenger-guests) and the very last to carry three classes: first, cabin and third class.

When Royal Mail decided to retire and then replace the last of its pre-war Highland class of liners – the *Highland Brigade, Highland Chieftain, Highland Monarch* and *Highland Princess* – and then reassign the larger *Andes* to fulltime cruising, company directors and designers agreed upon three, rather modern and in fact noteworthy passenger-cargo liners as replacements. The year was 1958.

Firstly, the new trio would abandon the Highland naming pattern and instead use three geographic selections: *Amazon, Aragon* and *Arlanza*. Secondly, in something of a throwback to the past, designers decided upon a 'break' in the superstructure; a split between the bridge and officers' quarters and the more extensive passenger accommodations. Overall, the new liners were also very much in the combo style; combination passenger and cargo – five cargo holds and a full capacity of 449 passengers.

The trio was ordered from the famed Harland & Wolff yard at Belfast and represented a total investment of $60 million. Their creation actually began in something of a final 'golden age' for the British passenger liner industry. Just across the ways at Belfast, P&O's 44,000-ton *Canberra* was taking shape. She would be Britain's largest liner in some twenty years, since the 83,000-ton *Queen Elizabeth* of 1940. Further away, across the Irish Sea at Birkenhead, the Cammell Laird yards were hard at work on the 37,000-ton *Windsor Castle*;

the largest liner ever for the South African trade. At Barrow-in-Furness, the 41,000-ton *Oriana* was soon to be launched, and then establish herself as the fastest liner ever on the Australian run. Then, as if for good measure, Union-Castle had also contracted for the 32,000-ton *Transvaal Castle* from the John Brown yard at Clydebank. Meanwhile, Shaw Savill had ordered the 24,000-ton *Northern Star*, Canadian Pacific was preparing for its new flagship *Empress of Canada* and all while Cunard was planning for a possible 75,000-tonner, dubbed the Q3, that would replace the aging *Queen Mary*. All seemed well and prosperous in the British ocean liner trade.

The 584-foot-long *Amazon* was the first of the three new Royal Mail liners to come off the ways, on 7 July 1959. HRH Princess Margaret did the naming. The *Aragon* followed on 20 October and then the *Arlanza* on 13 April 1960. Their maiden voyages had a similarly paced pattern: the *Amazon* made hers in January 1960, the *Aragon* in April and the *Arlanza* in October. Descriptive literature heralded the ships as 'the Three Graces'.

John Draffin worked in the Purser's Department on the *Amazon* and recalled the 20,400-ton ship with great fondness: 'The *Amazon* and her sisters were most distinctive and contemporary. They were, in fact, the first ships to have escalators. They were very much class-divided ships, however. The first class quarters were very deluxe, even despite the extensive use of modern materials. Second class was less fancy. The third class section was clean, but very simple. In third class, the waiters would dish out the food to twenty or twenty passengers at a table and then join them. Royal Mail employed Spanish and Portuguese staff for third class. Entertainment was different and, of course, limited. While first class passengers might be having a film, second class would have bingo and third class a quiz. Other entertainment in the Sixties on the *Amazon* might include a fashion show, horse-racing, dances and concerts with records.'

These Royal Mail sisters used the port of London as their northern terminus and sailed onwards via Cherbourg to Vigo, Lisbon, Las Palmas, Rio de Janeiro, Santos, Montevideo and finally Buenos Aires. The homeward voyage was identical, except that Boulogne was substituted for Cherbourg. Passenger loads were derived from a variety of sources including round-trip, cruise-like voyages. In 1966, the seven-week round-trip sailings were offered at barges, beginning at £391 in first class, £272 in cabin class and £182 in third class. Other traffic came from particularly high loads of one-way traffic to and from South America. Of special importance was the southbound migrant trade from Vigo and Lisbon, which used only the third class quarters. There was also a British tourist trade for the short-distance runs 'to the sun', to Spain, Portugal and the Canaries. The northbound, homeward voyages were less crowded; particularly in third class.

John Draffin also recalled the specialized sailing patterns of these ships and their revenue requirements: 'Being fast ships as well as good 'sea boats', but always tending to list somewhat, they were especially designed with shallow draughts for the River Plate. After the ten-day turnaround at Buenos Aires, where the ships loaded the chilled beef for shipment to Britain, they had to make the return sailing within three weeks, which was the limit for the beef. We would repeat the same ports of call mostly, but often returned to Southampton [instead of London] to offload our passengers, and then went to Rotterdam to discharge our European cargo before terminating the voyage at London, where the ships remained for ten days. The schedules were maintained like clockwork and each aspect of this extensive operation had a pattern. For example, always on the first day out of Rio, stowaways on the northbound ship were exchanged with her southbound sister ship.'

Bob Cummins also served on the *Amazon*. 'Then a brand-new beauty [1961], she had the finest first class restaurant I've ever seen and which catered for all of the hundred or so first class passengers at a single sitting. We'd have older British diplomats, the Argentine land barons and aristocracy, wealthy Britons and some well-heeled round-trippers. There were 91 berths in first class, 82 in cabin class and then 275 in third class. We took on the outbound passengers at the Tilbury Landing Stage. They had come down by train from London. We had a short tender call at Cherbourg. In South America, after landing passengers at Buenos Aires and sending the round-trippers either to hotels or on extended excursions, the ship was moved to La Plata for five days to load the very important Argentine beef. We would then return to Buenos Aires, take on the passengers, and then reverse the same route. Unfortunately, British labour problems killed these fine sister ships. Often, because of dockers' strikes and disruptions at London, we would return with half the cargo we brought up because of some problem on the London Docks. As late examples of combination passenger-cargo ships, they never quite made it. Even later, when they were transferred within the Furness Withy Group to Shaw Savill, they were equally unsuccessful.'

'In retrospect, the *Amazon* and her sisters were somewhat late for the South American passenger run, which was typically being overtaken by the airlines in the 1960s and all while the cargo side of their operations were complicated by more and more strikes, and often in the port of London,' noted Ron Peach. 'Once the London dockers had been on yet another long strike and refused to unload ships such as these. Royal Mail was not only beginning to lose patience, but lots of money as well.'

The 'Three Graces' survived for nearly a decade. After the devastating British maritime strike of 1966, when they were moored together in the London Docks, they began to suffer from the ills suffered by so many traditional passenger ships. There were operational problems, high operating costs, increased competition from the airlines, and new and more efficient cargo shipping methods. But then there was a final blow: the once lucrative Argentine beef trade collapsed and cast a deep, decisive blow to the UK–east coast of South America trade.

The *Amazon*, the first of the three sisters, was in fact the first to go. She was transferred, in February 1968, to Shaw Savill, promptly renamed *Akaroa* and dispatched on their around-the-world and Australia/New Zealand services. The other sisters were soon to follow. The *Aragon* was laid up for some time in Cornwall's River Fal, which was fast becoming something of a holding zone; a sort of 'maritime limbo' for out-of-work British passenger ships. She was passed to Shaw Savill in February 1969 and then hoisted her colours as the *Arawa*. The *Aragon*, the last to remain with Royal Mail, actually terminated the company's South American passenger service when she arrived at the London Docks on 21 February 1969. She too was transferred to Shaw Savill and was renamed *Aranda*. A long and distinguished and history-filled era had ended. Royal Mail's passenger operations survived thereafter for only two more years, ending when the *Andes* was retired in the spring of 1971.

The big British maritime strike of May–June 1966 was a crashing blow to the likes of the Royal Mail Lines. Ships like the *Aragon* were laid up, missing sailings and revenue. (Royal Mail Lines)

Changing hands: the *Aranda* (ex-*Aragon*) in Shaw Savill colours. (Author's Collection)

Different look: the *Hoegh Traveler* – ex-*Aragon*, ex-*Aranda* – being fitted-out as a car carrier at Rijeka in 1972. The Soviet liner *Rossia* is behind. (Hoegh-Ugland)

According to John Draffin, who served as a purser aboard both Royal Mail and Shaw Savill liners, 'While Furness Withy acquired Royal Mail in the mid-1960s, including their passenger fleet of four liners, they were, as parents, always more interested in Shaw Savill. After the big losses in the Argentine beef trade, with often delayed and sometimes near-empty sailings [in 1967–68], yet all while attempting to maintain a passenger schedule, the three 'A sisters' of Royal Mail might have been sold, but were retained and transferred to Shaw Savill. Unfortunately, it was a highly unsuccessful decision. The three 'A sisters' were made one-class [for approximately 470 passengers], but having originally been originally three-class in design and layout, now seemed 'chopped-up', with too many small lounges and public areas. Furthermore, by the late 1960s, Shaw Savill's passenger operation was no longer at its best.'

The rather large cargo capacity on the three ships, particularly with their extensive refrigerated space, was useful for the long-haul meat trades out of Australia and New Zealand. Mostly, they joined the liners *Northern Star* and *Southern Cross*, and sailed on world voyages: from London and/or Southampton, the usual itinerary being to the Azores, Barbados, Trinidad, Curaçao, the Panama Canal, Tahiti, Auckland, Wellington, Sydney, Melbourne, Fremantle, Durban, Cape Town and Las Palmas. Sometimes, the itinerary was reversed and at other times the ports of call varied. They was even occasional cruising, from Australia and New Zealand on short runs in the South Pacific. But, unfortunately, more hard times – especially financial ones – were ahead.

The *Akaroa* (ex-*Amazon*) was seriously damaged by fire at sea while some 1,000 miles south-west of the Azores on 15 April 1970. She limped back to Britain for repairs. But, within a year, rumours hinted that the three ships were again unprofitable, and were for sale.

The ships were out of place in the rapidly changing patterns of worldwide shipping. One rumour, which emerged in the spring of 1971, suggested that the *Akaroa* would be sold and converted to a floating hotel and moored in the Seychelles. Nothing came to pass. Shortly thereafter, the threesome was abruptly withdrawn from service.

Now, with Shaw Savill facing major losses, there was little time spent in waiting and idleness. The trio was sold for $700,000 – or just above their combined scrap value – to Norwegian buyers; the *Akaroa* to A/S Uglands Rederi and the *Aranda* and *Arawa* to Leif Hoegh & Company. Their futures represented a joint venture: for a total of $8 million, they would be converted to car carriers. The *Akaroa*, which was renamed *Akarita*, was sent to Grimstad for conversion. The *Aranda*, which became the *Hoegh Traveler*, and the *Arawa*, which changed to *Hoegh Transit*, sailed to the Viktor Lenac Shipyard at Rijeka in Yugoslavia.

It was surely the first time that deep-sea passenger ships had found new life as car carriers. All of the cargo holds were gutted and changed into vehicle stowage spaces. The passenger quarters were also removed and so left the three ships almost unrecognisable. However, some of the original first class cabins were retained for officers and crew, as were the original funnels. The bridge and wheelhouse sections were moved a long way forward, to a position above what had previously been the first cargo hold. Overall, the ships became almost bulky, floating sheds – undoubtedly 'working ships' – with little hint of any sleekness in design. Each ship's tonnage dropped from 20,000 to 11,000 tons and their capacities were listed as 3,000 cars rather than passengers per ship. Upon completion, they were assigned to the worldwide Hoegh-Ugland car-carrying trades. The author has seen at least two since their conversion, at Port Newark, New Orleans, Yokohama and in the upper reaches of the Hudson River near Yonkers, New York.

Their subsequent and final histories included further changes. The *Hoegh Transit* (ex-*Arlanza*, ex-*Arawa*) became the *Hoegh Trotter* within a year following her conversion by the Norwegians. All three ships changed hands in 1978. The *Akarita* (ex-*Amazon*, ex-*Akaroa*) went to Sagitta (Liberia) Ltd, under Liberian colours and became the *Hual Akarita*. The *Hoegh Traveler* (ex-*Aragon*, ex-*Aranda*) and the *Hoegh Trotter* both transferred to Ace Navigation Co. Ltd, also hoisting Liberian colours, and became the *Hual Traveler* and *Hual Trotter* respectively. In 1981, there were still further amendments. The *Hual Akarita* reverted to the name *Akarita* while the *Hual Traveler* became the *Traveler* and the *Hoegh Trotter* the *Trotter*.

In 1976, each of the ships passed their five-year surveys. But as the shipping scene continued to change and evolve, with both fluctuations in trading requirements and the continued emphasis on operational efficiency, the three ships were given a quite different evaluation. Evidently, they were no longer needed – or economically viable. The *Traveler* (ex-*Aragon*) departed from New Orleans in October 1981, bound for the scrapyards of Kaohsiung on Taiwan. The *Trotter* (ex-*Arlanza*) followed in December and finally the *Akarita* (ex-*Amazon*), last of the original trio, went her way in January.

11. Post Script: Long After Royal Mail

Royal Mail Lines, especially with the likes of the *Atlantis* and later the *Andes*, helped lay the foundation for today's British cruise industry. It is booming. Over 2½ million British travellers take cruises annually, and often from Southampton. While I have attempted to review the past – with histories of Royal Mail passenger ships – the era of passenger shipping continues, thrives and has a most positive future. In 2016 alone, no less than fifty-five cruise ships were being built or on the drawing boards. The likes of the *Andes* were a beginning to today's booming cruise trades.

Royal Mail Lines itself is but a memory – a long-ago maritime memory. By the mid-1960s, shipping patterns were clearly changing. In particular, the South American passenger trade was in deep decline; the airlines took passengers and freighters were gradually being replaced by larger, more efficient container ships. Matters were complicated further by the rapidly increasing costs of operating British-flag ships. The six-week British maritime strike, in May–June 1966, was extremely decisive. With rising rates for seamen and other demands, companies such as Royal Mail had to re-think their position and their future. Any thoughts of replacing the twenty-five-year-old *Andes*, for example, were stalled, while the future of the *Amazon*, *Arlanza* and *Aragon* was slipping deeper and deeper into question. Reorganisation and merger became the orders of the day. Royal Mail Lines was bought by another British ship-owner; the Furness Withy Group, in 1965. But there were further changes ahead. In the mid-1970s, the entire Furness Withy Group, including Royal Mail, was sold to the ever-expanding Hong Kong-based ship-owner C. Y. Tung. Later, however, Tung sold off his Furness Withy holdings to an earlier South American competitor; West Germany's Hamburg-Sud, the Hamburg-South America Line. By then without ships, Royal Mail was merely a name, and so had disappeared entirely from the sea lanes. This book has been created as a reminder of a great company and a glorious collection of passenger ships.

Bibliography

Baker, Rodney & Leonard, Alan, *Great Steamers White & Gold: A History of Royal Mail Ships & Services*, Southampton: Ensign Publications Ltd, 1993.

Braynard, Frank O. & Miller, William H., *Fifty Famous Liners* (Vol. I), Cambridge: Patrick Stephens Ltd, 1982.

Bushnell, T. A., *Royal Mail: A Centenary History of the Royal Mail Line 1839–1939*, London: Trade and Travel Publications Ltd, 1939.

Haws, Duncan, *Merchant Fleets: Royal Mail Line & Nelson Line*, Crowborough, Sussex: TCL Publications, 1982.

Miller, William H., *The Cruise Ships*, London: Conway Maritime Press Ltd, 1988.

Miller, William H., *The Last Blue Water Liners*, London: Conway Maritime Press Ltd, 1986.

Miller, William H., *Pictorial Encyclopedia of Ocean Liners 1860–1994*, Mineola, New York: Dover Publications Inc., 1995.

Nicol, Stuart, *MacQueen's Legacy: Ships of the Royal Mail Line, Volume II*, Stroud, Gloucestershire: Tempus Publishing Ltd, 2001.

Plowman, Peter, *Australian Migrant Ships 1946–77*, Sydney: Rosenberg Publishing Pty Ltd, 2006.